THE ETERNAL SONSHIP OF CHRIST

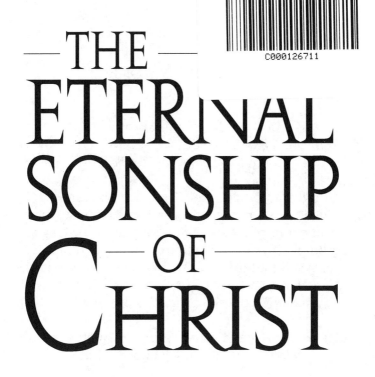

GEORGE W. ZELLER
RENALD E. SHOWERS

LOIZEAUX BROTHERS
Neptune, New Jersey

THE ETERNAL SONSHIP OF CHRIST
© 1993 by George Zeller

A Publication of Loizeaux Brothers, Inc.,
*A Nonprofit Organization Devoted to the Lord's Work
and to the Spread of His Truth.*

Unless otherwise indicated, Scripture quotations are
taken from the King James version.

Library of Congress Cataloging-in-Publication Data

Zeller, George W., 1950-
The eternal sonship of Christ / George Zeller, Renald Showers.
Includes bibliographical references.
ISBN 0-87213-986-7 (pbk.)
1. Jesus Christ—Divinity. 2. Son of God.
I. Showers, Renald E.   II. Title.
BT216.Z45 1993   93-21326
232'.8—dc20

Printed in the United States of America.

10 9 8 7 6 5 4 3 2 1

DEDICATION

Amidst unceasing cries for peace, love, tolerance, and unity, the discerning man of God knows that purity, truth, and sound doctrine are essential ingredients for a clear, vibrant testimony and for dynamic, Christ-honoring living. God's truth must never be sacrificed or compromised. This book is dedicated to the remnant of faithful, God-fearing believers who in these last days are "valiant for the truth upon the earth" (Jeremiah 9:3). May God give us grace to stand, to understand, and to withstand!

Crown Him the Son of God

Before the worlds began.

From the Hymn "Crown Him With Many Crowns"
by Matthew Bridges and Godfrey Thring

CONTENTS

FOREWORD

The true church of our Lord Jesus Christ is built on the believing confession of this divinely revealed and infinitely precious truth: "Thou art the Christ, the Son of the living God" (Matthew 16:16). This statement, revealed to the apostle Peter by God the Father, came in response to our Lord's question, "Whom say ye that I am?"

By definition an evangelical Christian affirms, among other things, the absolute and eternal deity of our Lord Jesus Christ. But Satan, the archenemy of God's people, is determined to confuse our understanding of this foundational truth and undermine our commitment to it. I, together with the authors of this book, believe that understanding and commitment are beginning to wane in connection with the question of the eternal Sonship of Jesus Christ our Lord.

If the second person of the triune godhead was not the Son of God until His incarnation, as some are now teaching, then the first person was not the Father until nearly two thousand years ago. One evangelical theologian who held this view recently speculated that "when the divine decision was made with regard to the incarnation, any of the three members of the Trinity could have accepted the various roles."[1] One wonders how according to this view there could even be first, second, and third persons in the godhead. One heresy seems to invite another.

And there *is* another. If the second person did not become the Son of God until the incarnation, was He truly deity before that moment? This question is highly relevant because, as the authors of this book have convincingly shown (from such passages as John 5:18; 10:30-39; 19:7), the Jews clearly understood Jesus' claim to be the Son of God to be a claim to absolute deity, "making himself equal with God" (John 5:18).

All such dangerous speculations have been swept away by George W. Zeller and Renald E. Showers in their masterful presentation of the eternal Sonship of Christ our Lord. They have demonstrated that even such familiar and precious verses as John 3:16 become almost meaningless if the Father was not the Father and the Son was not the Son until the incarnation. "For God so loved the world, that he gave his only begotten Son," Scripture tells us. How could the Father have done this if He had no Son to give?

May God be pleased to use this book to uplift the hearts of His people everywhere to worship, honor, and serve the eternal Father, the eternal Son, and the eternal Holy Spirit—one God—blessed forever.

John C. Whitcomb
Winona Lake, Indiana

PREFACE

And we know that the Son of God is come, and hath given us an understanding, that we may know him that is true, and we are in him that is true, even in his Son Jesus Christ. This is the true God, and eternal life (1 John 5:20).

I n writing this volume the authors are fully persuaded that the Bible is the written Word of God, inerrant and absolutely infallible. God's Word is the only valid source of information concerning the existence and character of God and the origin and destiny of man. In humbleness of heart and with childlike faith we should submit to God's revelation of Himself: "All things are delivered unto me of my Father: and no man knoweth the Son, but the Father; neither knoweth any man the Father, save the Son, and he to whomsoever the Son will reveal him" (Matthew 11:27).

The Bible reveals among other things that God has graciously made full provision for man's salvation in and through His only-begotten unique Son, our Lord Jesus Christ. It is the desire of God that redeemed man should worship, honor, love, and serve Him. As the Westminster *Shorter Catechism* says, "Man's chief end is to glorify God, and to enjoy Him for ever."

A correct understanding of God's revelation of Himself is vital if we are to respond properly to God in worship, love, and praise. One of the most remarkable truths revealed in the Bible is the triune nature of the godhead— God the Father, God the Son, and God the Holy Spirit.

These three persons of the godhead are one in the essential being of God, and yet each person is carefully distinguished in the Scriptures. Each person of the triune godhead has unique glories that rightly apprehended increase our love and admiration for our great God.

The Bible reveals that in the godhead exists a very special relationship that is implicit in the names *Father* and *Son*. We believe the Scriptures clearly teach that this relationship is of an eternal nature and that it displays one of the most beautiful and appealing glories of the Lord Jesus Christ, one that should delight our hearts and inspire our worship.

Over the years many have denied the eternal Sonship of Christ. Their reasons are basically twofold: (1) they feel that the term *Son* denotes inferiority and subjection, characteristics felt to be inappropriate to our understanding of the essential and eternal nature of Christ; (2) they speculate that the relationships between the persons of the godhead revealed in the New Testament were not actually personalized until the time of Christ's incarnation or even later. The position of those who deny the eternal Sonship of Christ will be referred to in this book as the incarnational Sonship view.

The differences between the two positions are significant. These differences are not simply matters of semantics or mere theological technicalities; they are fundamental. The following chart helps to summarize and contrast the two positions:

ETERNAL SONSHIP	INCARNATIONAL SONSHIP
He was always the Son of God. He is the eternal Son.	Before the incarnation He was not the Son of God.
"Son of God" is **Who He Is**.	"Son of God" is **What He Became.**

ETERNAL SONSHIP	INCARNATIONAL SONSHIP
His Sonship is essential to His true identity and cannot be divorced from the person that He is.	His Sonship is not essential to His inherent identity.
"Son of God" is who He is in His being of beings.	"Son of God" is merely a title and role that He assumed.
His Sonship directly relates to His deity.	His Sonship directly relates to His incarnation.
"Son of God" means equal with God, indicating likeness or sameness of being.	"Son of God" means subservient to God, less than God.
God the Father has always been God the Father.	God the Father did not assume the title and role of Father until the incarnation.
Before the incarnation the Son was ever in the Father's bosom.	Before the incarnation God had no Son, nor was He the Father.
The Father/Son relationship has eternally existed in the godhead.	Before the incarnation there was no Father/Son relationship in the godhead.
The Father sent His own Son into this world (see John 3:16-17; Galatians 4:4; etc.).	The One who would become the Father sent the One who would become the Son into this world.
The triune God has eternally existed in three persons—Father, Son, and Holy Spirit.	The triune God has eternally existed in three persons, but not as Father, Son, and Holy Spirit. These were roles that were assumed in time.

The authors are concerned because many believers, when confronted with these two positions, do not see the importance of the issue.

Years ago one of this century's great preachers, Dr. H. A. Ironside, wrote a history of the Plymouth Brethren movement. In this volume he mentioned an American Bible teacher, a follower of F. E. Raven, who denied eternal Sonship:

> More recently the so-called Raven meetings have been divided over the teaching of an American leader who denied the truth of the Eternal Sonship of Christ. This most serious error caused many to take a definite stand against it and led to another separation. But sadly enough by far the greater majority saw nothing wrong in such views and have gone on with the promulgator of them. This puts these meetings entirely off the ground of the early Brethren who considered a true confession of Christ the very first consideration.[1]

Several observations should be made: (1) Dr. Ironside, recognized as a man of keen doctrinal discernment, considered the denial of eternal Sonship a "most serious error"; (2) some took a definite stand against this error and a separation resulted; (3) Dr. Ironside was grieved not because of the necessary separation, but because "the greater majority saw nothing wrong" with such teaching and they continued to follow this Bible teacher; (4) Dr. Ironside as well as the early Brethren considered the denial of eternal Sonship to be incompatible with "a true confession of Christ."

History often repeats itself. Today there is a similar situation that is of grave concern to the authors and numerous others. When confronted with the denial of eternal Sonship, too many believers, including pastors and other Christian leaders, do not understand the importance of the issue. They do not consider the denial serious error. They see nothing wrong with it. In their way of thinking it does not significantly affect the true doctrine of Christ, and the issue is certainly not worth fighting over. They are grieved not because of the error that is allowed and propagated, but because of those voices who seek to proclaim and preserve the doctrine of eternal Sonship. Those who speak out are criticized for their lack of love and tolerance and for causing discord among brethren.

In writing this book the desire of the authors is not to divide brethren, but rather to unite believers on the basis of a common understanding of the blessed person of the Son of God "till we all come in the unity of the faith, and of the knowledge of the Son of God, unto a perfect man, unto the measure of the stature of the fulness of Christ" (Ephesians 4:13). This book seeks to show from the Scriptures the divine character of Christ and the eternal nature of the relationship between God the Father and God the Son. This book also seeks to alert believers against any teaching that would in any way detract from the glory of God's eternal and beloved Son.

The doctrine of the eternal Sonship of Christ cannot be set aside or minimized for the following reasons: (1) it is a doctrine plainly taught in the Word of God; (2) the teaching that denies the eternal Sonship of Christ robs the body of Christ, the true church, of a vital and precious belief essential to a proper understanding and appreciation of His person and work; (3) the truth of the gospel message and its presentation are affected because if we are not proclaiming Christ as the eternal Son of God, then we are preaching a Savior other than the person who has been revealed in the Scriptures; (4) failure to understand the persons of the godhead as revealed by His Word limits one's practical relationship to His triune being; (5) denial of eternal Sonship deprives us of the enjoyment of one of the most beautiful glories of the Lord Jesus Christ.

In this book George Zeller first establishes the deity of Christ and His pre-existence, after which he briefly examines the significance of the incarnation. Then he explains the doctrine of eternal Sonship and contrasts this position with the incarnational Sonship view.

The defense of the doctrine of eternal Sonship begins in chapter 6 with an examination by Mr. Zeller of the clear Scriptural evidence in support of the truth that the Father/Son relationship existed long before Bethlehem. The following chapter, written by Renald Showers, shows the Biblical significance of the term *Son of God* and demonstrates that it cannot mean "subservient to God." Next is his detailed examination of Psalm 2:7, which is a critical Old Testament passage relating to Sonship; Dr. Showers considers this verse in light of its context and its New Testament usage.

Certain passages in God's Word seem to some to support the incarnational Sonship position; in chapter 9 Mr. Zeller discusses these passages and analyzes some of the other arguments used by opponents of eternal Sonship. In the final chapter he explains why this doctrine is so important and necessary and why it must be upheld and defended by God's people.

Dr. Herbert Bess, a Hebrew scholar, has graciously granted the authors permission to include in appendix A the excellent article in which he demonstrates that the true significance of the term *Son of God* is based on a very common Hebrew and Semitic idiom. His research gives further Biblical evidence supporting the conclusions of this book. In appendix B Mr. Zeller quotes other Bible teachers on the subject of eternal Sonship.

It is the great desire of the authors that readers of this book might be better enabled to praise and worship God as they contemplate the enormity of Christ's condescension. The eternal Son emptied Himself and humbled Himself and became poor so that He might taste death for every man, thereby making it possible for the believing sinner to be made rich in Him (2 Corinthians 8:9). May the living God ever receive our glory, honor, and praise: "Now unto the King eternal, immortal, invisible, the only wise God, be honour and glory for ever and ever. Amen" (1 Timothy 1:17).

George Zeller
Renald Showers

Chapter 1

THE DEITY OF THE SON

In the beginning was the Word, and the Word was with God, and the Word was God (John 1:1).

Make no mistake about it. The infallible Word of God clearly identifies Jesus Christ as God. He is "the great God" (Titus 2:13), "the mighty God" (Isaiah 9:6), and "the true God" (1 John 5:20). Full and complete deity is ascribed to Him: "The Word was God" (John 1:1). Although a Jew according to the flesh, He is the One "who is over all, God blessed for ever" (Romans 9:5).[1]

To know Jesus Christ is to know God (John 14:8-9). To see Jesus Christ is to see God: "He that hath seen me hath seen the Father" (John 14:9). Christ is the "image of the invisible God" (Colossians 1:15), "the brightness of his glory, and the express image of his person" (Hebrews 1:3). "In him dwelleth all the fulness of the Godhead bodily" (Colossians 2:9). "All men should honour the Son, even as they honour the Father" (John 5:23). We honor the Father as God, and we must honor the Son in the same way. The Son of God is not honored when His deity is denied.

Witnesses to Christ's deity are many. Peter referred to Jesus Christ as God (2 Peter 1:1).[2] The apostle Paul declared Christ's deity in several places (Titus 2:13; Philippians 2:6; Romans 9:5). Isaiah identified the Messiah as God (Isaiah 7:14; 9:6). Worshiping the risen Lord, Thomas said, "My Lord and my God" (John 20:28) and Jesus did not rebuke him for this. What Thomas said was true.

Because Jesus Christ is God, He is all that God is. The Lord Jesus fully possesses all the attributes of deity. He is holy (Luke 1:35), righteous (1 John 2:1), eternal (Micah 5:2), unchangeable (Hebrews 13:8), omnipotent (Revelation 1:8; 22:12-13), omnipresent (Matthew 28:20), and omniscient (John 2:24-25; 6:64; 16:30). Every attribute that belongs to the Father belongs to the Son: "All things that the Father hath are mine" (John 16:15).

Because Jesus Christ is God, He can perform works that only God can do. Only God is the Creator, and the Bible declares that by the Son all things were created (John 1:3; Colossians 1:16). Only God can forgive sins, and Jesus Christ forgave sins (Mark 2:5-7). Only God answers prayer, and the Lord Jesus said, "If ye shall ask any thing in my name, I will do it" (John 14:14). Only God will sit on the final throne of judgment, and the Scriptures identify Jesus Christ as the final judge of all men (John 5:22,27).

Cults and liberal theologians commonly deny the full deity of Jesus Christ. Unbelieving hearts refuse to face up to who He really is.

The term *God* (the Hebrew *Elohim*) may be applied to the true God (Genesis 1:1) and also to false gods (Exodus 20:3). However, the sacred name *Jehovah* (written in capital letters as LORD or GOD in the Old Testament) is applicable to none but deity. It is derived from the verb *to be* and communicates that Jehovah is the One who was, who is, and who ever shall be (Revelation 1:8). The Lord Himself jealously guards this name and all that it stands for, as seen in the following two passages: Psalm 83:18, "That men may know that thou, whose name alone is JEHOVAH, art the most high over all the earth"; and Isaiah 42:8, "I am the LORD: that is my name: and my glory will I not give to another." Thus no greater proof of deity could be presented concerning Christ than that He should rightfully be called Jehovah.

Consider the following evidence that the Lord Jesus Christ is rightfully called Jehovah:

1. In Zechariah 12 Jehovah is speaking (see verses 1 and 4). In verse 10 Jehovah says, "They shall look upon me whom they have pierced." This can refer to no one but Christ (John 19:37 and Revelation 1:7).

2. Jehovah of the Old Testament declares Himself to be the first and the last (Isaiah 44:6). In the New Testament Jesus Christ is said to be the first and the last (Revelation 1:8,11,17-18; 22:13).

3. In Isaiah 6:5 the prophet said, "Mine eyes have seen the King, the LORD [Jehovah] of hosts." Isaiah saw Jehovah! The apostle John referred to this event in John 12:41 and made it clear that the person whom Isaiah saw was actually Jesus Christ: "These things said Esaias [Isaiah], when he saw his [Christ's] glory, and spake of him."

4. In Psalm 23:1 David declared that Jehovah is the great Shepherd of the sheep. The New Testament identifies Jesus Christ as the great Shepherd of the sheep (Hebrews 13:20; John 10:11,14).

5. The Old Testament repeatedly refers to Jehovah as Israel's Rock (Deuteronomy 32:3-4,18; Psalm 18:2; 62:1-2). The New Testament clearly identifies this Rock as Christ (1 Corinthians 10:4).

6. Jehovah declares Himself to be the only Savior (Isaiah 43:10-11; 45:21). There is no Savior apart from Him! In the New Testament Peter declared that Jesus is the only Savior (Acts 4:12). In Isaiah 45:22 Jehovah says, "Look unto me, and be ye saved . . . there is none else." In John 3:14-16 we are told to look unto the crucified One to be saved.

7. In Isaiah 45:23 Jehovah says, "That unto me every knee shall bow, every tongue shall swear." This passage is applied to Christ in Philippians 2:9-11. He is the One before whom all will someday bow. Every tongue will confess that Jesus Christ is Lord.[3]

8. In Isaiah 24:23 and Zephaniah 3:15-17 we learn that Jehovah Himself will reign in Jerusalem during the coming kingdom age and He will be in the midst of His people. The

New Testament clearly identifies this future, millennial King as Jesus Christ (Revelation 19:11-16; 20:4,6).

9. In Isaiah 40:3 we read that the forerunner was to prepare the way for the coming of Jehovah. The same passage is applied to Christ in Mark 1:1-3. John the Baptist prepared the way for Christ.

10. Isaiah 8:13-14 prophetically states that "the LORD" (Jehovah) will be "for a stone of stumbling and for a rock of offence." These verses are applied to Jesus Christ in 1 Peter 2:7-8.

11. In Psalm 34:8 we are invited to taste and see that Jehovah is good. This passage is clearly alluded to in 1 Peter 2:3. Referring to the goodness and graciousness of Jesus Christ, Peter wrote, "If so be ye have tasted that the Lord is gracious."

12. The Old Testament promises salvation and deliverance to those who call on the name of Jehovah (Joel 2:32). In the New Testament this passage is used to present a promise of salvation to all those who call on the name of the Lord Jesus Christ (Romans 10:13; Acts 2:21; also see Acts 2:36).

The above evidence shows beyond doubt that the name *Jehovah* may rightfully be applied to Jesus Christ.[4] Since this term is applicable only to deity and can rightfully be applied to Jesus Christ, we must conclude that the Lord Jesus is Jehovah God. He is the Son of God (Matthew 16:16) and He is God the Son (1 John 5:20; Hebrews 1:8). To Him be glory and honor, both now and forevermore![5]

Chapter 2

THE PRE-EXISTENCE
OF THE SON

*Jesus said unto them, Verily, verily, I say unto you,
Before Abraham was, I am (John 8:58).*

I f Jesus Christ is God, then He must be eternal. God has no beginning. There was never a time when He did not exist in all the fullness of who He is. "Before the mountains were brought forth, or ever thou hadst formed the earth and the world, even from everlasting to everlasting, thou art God" (Psalm 90:2).

Some heretical cults deny Christ's eternal existence, claiming that He was a created being. In contrast to this false doctrine, the Bible presents Him as the uncreated Creator: "All things were made by him; and without him was not any thing made that was made" (John 1:3). In the beginning, He was not created or made. In the beginning, He already was (John 1:1-2). The apostle Paul declared that "He is before all things" (Colossians 1:17).

The prophet Micah foretold that the Messiah would be born in the little town of Bethlehem. Who is this One who would be born? He is the One "whose goings forth have been from of old, from everlasting" (Micah 5:2).

John the Baptist clearly pointed to the fact of Christ's pre-existence: "John bare witness of him, and cried, saying, This was he of whom I spake, He that cometh after me is preferred before me: for he was before me" (John 1:15). We can only understand this paradoxical statement as we distinguish between the two natures of Christ. When viewed from the standpoint of His humanity, He came after John the Baptist. Mary gave birth to Him six months after Elizabeth gave birth to John (Luke 1:26). But as the eternal Son of God, Christ was before John the Baptist, eternally existing in the bosom of the Father (John 1:18).

Perhaps the Savior Himself made the clearest statement of His pre-existence. Speaking with a group of unbelieving Jewish religious leaders He said, "Your father Abraham rejoiced to see my day: and he saw it, and was glad." The Jews, understanding Jesus to be saying that He and Abraham existed on earth at the same time, were startled. "Then said the Jews unto him, Thou art not yet fifty years old, and hast thou seen Abraham?" They knew that Abraham had lived and died approximately two thousand years earlier. They were shocked and angered by the Lord's final words: "Jesus said unto them, Verily, verily, I say unto you, Before Abraham was, I am." They considered this to be ultimate blasphemy and "took . . . up stones to cast at him." (See John 8:56-59.)

Only the eternal God could make such a claim. Indeed, Jesus could have said, "Before Adam was, I am." He even could have said, "Before the universe was, I am." In fact, He did make such a statement: "And now, O Father, glorify thou me with thine own self with the glory which I had with thee before the world was. . . . for thou lovedst me before the foundation of the world" (John 17:5,24). God the Son basked in the sunlight of the Father's love before the world ever was. From everlasting to everlasting, He is the Son of the Father's love. The eternal Son is worthy of all glory, praise, and adoration!

Chapter 3

THE INCARNATION OF THE SON

*The Word was made flesh, and dwelt among us
(John 1:14).
God was manifest in the flesh
(1 Timothy 3:16).*

C ontemplate the wonder of the incarnation. The infi-
nite God became a man. The Bible describes it in
simple language: "The Word was God. . . . And the
Word was made [became] flesh, and dwelt among us" (John
1:1,14). The eternal One stepped into time (Galatians 4:4).
The God who never had a beginning and who always
existed was born as an infant (Micah 5:2; Isaiah 7:14; 9:6).
The Almighty rested in the arms of Mary as a dependent
baby. The Creator of all things lay in a receptacle built for
feeding animals (Luke 2:12). The One who was "high and
lifted up" (Isaiah 6:1) was greeted by lowly shepherds.

Perhaps the most wondrous fact of the incarnation is
that it made the death of the immortal One possible. Man's
sin deserved and demanded death (Romans 1:32; 6:23),
thus dooming man to an eternal destiny separated from the
God of life (Isaiah 59:2; 2 Thessalonians 1:8-9). So God
lovingly devised a way to provide salvation for sinful man
without compromising His just and righteous character.
Serving as man's substitute, He would Himself pay the

death penalty for sinful man. To do this, God must become a man "that he by the grace of God should taste death for every man" (Hebrews 2:9). The immortal One could not die, but God took upon Himself our humanity and the God-Man could die and did die for our sins (1 Corinthians 15:3; 1 Peter 3:18).

Yes, He was born to die. His purpose for coming into this world was to save sinners (1 Timothy 1:15; John 3:17). He accomplished this saving work not in Bethlehem's cradle, but on Golgotha's cross. His birth made His death possible; His death made our salvation possible. The Bible describes it this way: "For ye know the grace of our Lord Jesus Christ, that, though he was rich, yet for your sakes he became poor, that ye through his poverty might be rich" (2 Corinthians 8:9).

Let no one misunderstand the significance of the incarnation. God became flesh, and God became a man, but He did not become the Son. He became a partaker of flesh and blood and was made like His brethren (Hebrews 2:14,17), but He did not become the Son of God by His incarnation. John taught that the eternal Word became *flesh* (John 1:1,14). Paul used similar language to communicate the fact that the Son "was made of the seed of David according to the flesh" (Romans 1:3). He who always was the Son of God became the Son of David by human birth. The eternal God became a man, born of the house and lineage of David. The eternal God did not become the Son of God.

The Lord Jesus once posed a question to the Pharisees that they could not answer: "What think ye of Christ [the Messiah]? whose son is he? They say unto him, The Son of David. He saith unto them . . . If David then call him Lord [in Psalm 110:1]; how is he his son?" (Matthew 22:42-45). The Pharisees were silenced by this question, but years later another Pharisee, Paul, whose eyes had been opened by God's grace, gave the answer. Paul preached the gospel of God that centered in "his Son Jesus Christ our Lord, which was made of the seed of David according to the flesh; And declared to be the Son of God with power, according to the spirit of holiness, by the resurrection from the dead" (Romans 1:3-4). In His humanity He is the Son of David. In His deity He is the Son of God and thus is David's Lord. His resurrection was the final proof that He was everything He claimed to be.

The Lord Jesus Christ did not become God at the incarnation, nor did the incarnation mark the beginning of His divine Sonship. The incarnation was the point in time at which God's eternal Son assumed our humanity without ceasing to be God. The Son of God became the Son of man, that we, the sons of men, might become the sons of God (John 1:12; Galatians 3:26). May we ever be filled with wonder and praise because of the condescending love and grace by which He stooped so low in order to raise us so high. "Behold, what manner of love the Father hath bestowed upon us, that we should be called the sons of God" (1 John 3:1).

Chapter 4

THE DOCTRINE OF
ETERNAL SONSHIP

No man hath seen God at any time; the only begotten Son, the One ever being (existing) in the bosom of the Father, He hath declared Him (John 1:18, literal rendering from the Greek).

T he doctrine of eternal Sonship declares that the second person of the triune godhead has eternally existed as the Son. The inspired Scriptures clearly identify Him as the Son of God. There was never a time when He was not the Son of God. At the incarnation He became a man; He did not *become* the Son. He was, is, and ever will be the Son. Son of God is His essential and inherent identity: "And we believe and are sure that thou art that Christ, the Son of the living God" (John 6:69). These are solid, indisputable, Biblical facts on which the Christian faith may be fixed.

Those who deny this doctrine teach that Jesus *became* the Son of God at some point in history. Some say He became the Son at His baptism. Others say He became the Son at His resurrection, or even at His exaltation. Most of them, however, say He became the Son of God at the incarnation.[1] Regardless of different understandings concerning the time and event marking the beginning of His Sonship, those who deny the eternal Sonship of Christ all agree that there was a time when He was not the Son of God.

The controversy surrounding Christ's Sonship hinges on certain key questions: Has there always existed a Father/Son relationship between the first and second persons of the godhead? Is Sonship merely a role, title, or function that Christ assumed at some point in history or is He essentially and eternally the beloved Son of the Father? Is Jesus Christ the eternal Son of God, or did He become the Son of God at the incarnation? Is He the true, proper, and actual Son of God intrinsically? Was the Son of God always in the bosom of the Father (John 1:18)? Is it wrong to refer to Him as the only begotten of the Father prior to His conception at Nazareth and His birth at Bethlehem? Before the creation of the world was Christ the Son?

God's Word provides solid and satisfying answers to all such questions. We approach this study with much caution and reverence, for we are speaking of the blessed Son of God, our Savior and Lord. May we write nothing that would bring shame or dishonor to His holy name and to His blessed person.

"No man knoweth the Son, but the Father; neither knoweth any man the Father, save the Son, and he to whomsoever the Son will reveal him. . . . I thank thee, O Father, Lord of heaven and earth, because thou hast hid these things from the wise and prudent, and hast revealed them unto babes" (Matthew 11:27,25). May the Father open our eyes and clearly reveal these things to us that we might worship, adore, and serve His Son.

A detailed defense of the doctrine of eternal Sonship will be presented later. For now an overview of the evidence will suffice. We will begin our survey at the resurrection and go backward in time to before the world was created to see if we can find evidence showing that the second person of the Trinity existed as the Son.

At the resurrection Jesus Christ our Lord was "declared

to be the Son of God with power" (Romans 1:4). He did not become the Son at this point in time, but He demonstrated that He was the Son. The resurrection was the promised sign (John 2:18-19; Matthew 12:38-40) that vindicated His claims and proved He was exactly who He said He was.

Going further back in time, we come to the transfiguration when the Father spoke audibly and declared Christ's Sonship: "This is my beloved Son, in whom I am well pleased; hear ye him" (Matthew 17:5). Traveling back to the beginning of Jesus' public ministry, we hear a similar declaration on the occasion of His baptism: "And lo a voice from heaven, saying, This is my beloved Son, in whom I am well pleased" (Matthew 3:17).

The next stop in our trip backward through time will be at Jesus' birth. An angel spoke these words about the One who would be born: "Therefore also that holy thing which shall be born of thee shall be called the Son of God" (Luke 1:35). At His birth Jesus was Lord (Luke 2:11), King (Matthew 2:2), and Son of God (Luke 1:35)!

As we go back into the Lord's preincarnate history, is there any evidence that He was identified as God's Son? In John 16:28 the Lord Jesus said, "I came forth from the Father, and am come into the world." This passage clearly indicates that before coming into this world Jesus was with the Father, strongly implying that a Father/Son relationship existed prior to the incarnation. Also the many passages that speak of the Father sending the Son (John 3:17; Galatians 4:4, etc.) suggest that Jesus existed as the Son prior to His mission. The Father did not send One who would become His Son; He sent One who was already His Son into the world.

Do we find mention of the Son of God prior to the New Testament? The Old Testament says little about the distinct persons of the Trinity. Some passages, however, mention or at least hint at Christ's Sonship. Isaiah predicted that there would come a day when God's Son would be given. (Compare Isaiah 9:6 with John 3:16.) In Psalm 2:12 the kings of the earth are told to "kiss the Son." In Daniel 3:25 Nebuchadnezzar was astounded to see a fourth person in the fiery furnace, whose form "is like the Son of God." Regardless of Nebuchadnezzar's understanding of who was in that furnace, from our perspective we can identify that fourth person as the preincarnate Christ, God's unique Son.[2] Proverbs 30:4, another fascinating passage, speaks of the Creator and also the Creator's Son! These passages suggest that during the Old Testament period the idea of God having a Son could be found in the Scriptures, although the full revelation of this truth awaited the New Testament period.

Let us now go back to the time of creation. In Colossians 1:13-16 and Hebrews 1:2 we are told that all things were created by the Son. These passages point to the fact that Jesus was the Son of God at the time of creation. They do not say that all things were made by One who would become the Son of God at a later time.

Finally we come to the time before the universe existed. We can know nothing of this time apart from divine revelation. The Lord Jesus gave us a remarkable glimpse into those past ages of eternity in His prayer to the Father: "And now, O Father, glorify thou me with thine own self with the glory which I [the Son] had with thee [the Father] before the world was. . . . for thou [the Father] lovedst me [the Son] before the foundation of the world" (John 17:5,24).

We conclude that before the world existed, the Father and the Son had a marvelous love relationship. The eternal Son of God was ever the delight of His Father's heart. Before the foundation of the world, the only begotten of the Father was constantly abiding in the Father's bosom (John 1:18). We are reminded of the Father's words, "This is my beloved Son."

Chapter 5

THE DENIAL OF ETERNAL SONSHIP

We have seen and do testify that the Father sent the Son to be the Saviour of the world. Whosoever shall confess that Jesus is the Son of God, God dwelleth in him, and he in God (1 John 4:14-15).

The vital doctrine of the eternal Sonship of Christ is under attack today. Those who deny this doctrine teach that Jesus *became* the Son of God at some point in history. Some say He became the Son at His baptism. Others say He became the Son at His resurrection, or even at His exaltation. Most of them, however, say He became the Son of God at the incarnation. They believe that the Lord Jesus Christ, before His incarnation in the womb of the virgin Mary, was the eternal Word, the eternal God, and even the eternal second person of the Trinity, but He was not the eternal Son. He did not assume the role of Son or bear the name or title of Son, they believe, until the incarnation. Regardless of different understandings concerning the time and event marking the beginning of His Sonship, those who deny the eternal Sonship of Christ all agree that there was a time when He was not the Son of God.

Such teachers do not deny the deity of Christ, and for this we can be thankful. They do not deny the eternal existence of Christ or deny that three distinct persons in the

triune godhead have eternally existed. They teach that
Christ was always God but that He *became* the Son. According to this teaching, only when the Word became flesh
did He take on the role, function, and title of Son. Thus they
deny that He is essentially and eternally the Son of God.

A brief history of the controversy

Many years ago there was a great controversy, especially among the Plymouth Brethren assemblies, as to
whether the Lord Jesus was the Son throughout eternity or
whether He became Son at the time of His incarnation. An
influential teacher who denied the truth of His eternal
Sonship, F. E. Raven, made this statement in 1895: "Now,
'Son of God' I understand to be the title of Christ incarnate;
I should hardly use 'Son of God' as referring to His eternal
Person."[1] In contrast to this, Plymouth Brethren leaders
such as John Nelson Darby, William Kelly, and C. H. Mackintosh strongly defended the doctrine of eternal Sonship.[2]

This same controversy raged among some of the Bap-
tists. To resolve the dispute, J. C. Philpot wrote a ninety-
three-page defense of the doctrine of eternal Sonship. It is
a well-written, well-reasoned, and reverent study.[3]

Attacks on the doctrine of eternal Sonship are not new
and have come from a variety of sources. Theologians have
denied that Christ has eternally existed as the Son[4] and
noted commentators have taught the same.[5] A nationally
known television preacher also espoused this view.[6] *Dake's
Annotated Reference Bible* in its comment under Acts
13:33 strongly rejects the doctrine of eternal Sonship:

> As God, the person we now know of as Jesus Christ
> had no beginning, was not begotten, was not a Son,
> and did not come into being. . . . but as man and as
> God's Son He was not eternal, He did have a begin-
> ning, He was begotten, this being the same time
> Mary had a Son. Therefore, the doctrine of eternal

sonship of Jesus Christ is irreconcilable to reason, is unscriptural, and is contradictory to itself.[7]

A respected theologian and author of a classic book on the cults, Dr. Walter Martin, has also repudiated the doctrine of eternal Sonship:

> The Scripture nowhere calls Jesus Christ the eternal Son of God, and He is never called Son at all prior to the incarnation, except in prophetic passages in the Old Testament. The term "Son" itself is a functional term, as is the term "Father" and has no meaning apart from time. . . . Many heresies have seized upon the confusion created by the illogical "eternal Sonship" or "eternal generation" theory of Roman Catholic theology, unfortunately carried over to some aspects of Protestant theology. Finally; there cannot be any such thing as eternal Sonship. . . . the word "Son" definitely suggests inferiority.[8]

A more recent denial of the doctrine of eternal Sonship comes from the published writings of one of America's most popular Bible teachers, Dr. John MacArthur, Jr. In his commentary on the book of Hebrews he wrote:

> The Bible nowhere speaks of the eternal sonship of Christ. . . . He was always God, but He became **Son**. He had not always had the title of Son. That is His incarnation title. Eternally He is God, but only from His incarnation has He been Son. . . . Christ was **not** Son until His incarnation. Before that He was eternal God. It is therefore incorrect to say that Jesus Christ is eternally inferior to God because He goes under the title of Son. He is no "eternal Son" always subservient to God, always less than God, always under God. Sonship is an analogy to help us under-

stand Christ's essential relationship and willing submission to the Father for the sake of our redemption. As already mentioned, the **today** of verse 5 (Heb.1:5) shows that His sonship began in a point of time, not in eternity. His life as Son began in this world. . . . He was not a Son until He was born into this world through the virgin birth. . . . The sonship of Christ is inextricably connected with His incarnation [emphasis his].[9]

In his commentary on the book of Galatians, Dr. MacArthur made similar statements:

Some 900 years before Jesus was born God prophesied, "I will be a Father to Him, and He shall be a Son to Me" (Heb.1:5; 2 Sam. 7:14), indicating that in eternity past that [*sic*], though there were always three persons in the Trinity, there were not yet the roles of Father and Son. Those designations apparently came into being only at the incarnation. In the announcement of Jesus' birth to Mary, the angel Gabriel declared, "He will be great, and **will be called** the Son of the Most High . . . the holy offspring **shall be called** the Son of God" [Luke 1:32,35]. **Son** was a new name, never before applied to the second person of the Godhead except prophetically, as in Psalm 2:7, which is interpreted in Hebrews 1:5-6 as referring to the event of His incarnation. John wrote, "In the beginning was the Word, and the Word was with God, and the Word was God" (John 1:1). Only when "the Word became flesh, and dwelt among us" as "the only begotten God" (John 1:14,18) did He take on the role and function of **Son** [emphasis his].[10]

Dr. MacArthur has also published a commentary dealing with Romans 1 in which he again made his position on Sonship clear:

> Over the years, theologians have debated about whether Christ is the Son of God in eternity. Christ is and always has been the second member of the Trinity but only became a Son in His incarnation. When you think of the word **son** you probably think of the submission, obedience, and honor shown to one's father. That is the sense in which Jesus is the Son. Nowhere in Scripture does it say that Jesus has eternally been the Son. . . . From eternity He has been the second Person of the Trinity. He assumed the role of a Son in His incarnation.[11]

Dr. John MacArthur may be the best-known proponent of the Sonship-by-incarnation position, but he is by no means alone in holding this view. Many others do as well, including one professor from a prominent seminary who has carried this teaching to a dangerous extreme. In a letter to me he stated, "I know that hypotheses are problematic, but I have personally hypothesized that when the divine decision was made with regard to the incarnation, any of the three members of the Trinity could have accepted the various roles."[12] This means that the Father could have been the Son, the Son could have been the Spirit, the Spirit could have been the Father, etc. This is dangerous doctrine, but after all if Sonship and Fatherhood are merely assumed roles, then there is no reason for them not to have been interchangeable.

The position that Christ *became* the Son of God can be summarized as follows: (1) Nowhere in Scripture does it say that Jesus has eternally been the Son. (2) He was always God, the second person of the Trinity. (3) He became the Son at the time of the incarnation. (4) Sonship involves taking on a new function, receiving a title, and assuming a role that He previously did not have. (5) The main ideas conveyed by the term *Son* are those of submission, obedience, subservience, and even inferiority.

In sharp contrast to this, the doctrine of eternal Sonship affirms the following: (1) The Bible clearly teaches that Christ has eternally been the Son. (2) He was always God, the second person of the Trinity, **and He was always the Son of God.** (3) The eternal Son became man at the time of the incarnation. (4) Sonship involves the very person and nature of Jesus Christ, the essence of who He is as the second person of the Trinity, and thus there could never have been a time when He was not the Son because there could never have been a time when He was other than who He is. (5) The term *Son of God* indicates three things—(a) He is a person distinct from God His Father, (b) He is the heir, not the servant of His Father (*Son of God* does not mean "subservient to God"), and (c) He shares the divine nature of God His Father. The Biblical significance of the term *Son of God* will be developed further by Dr. Showers in chapter 7.

Chapter 6

THE DEFENSE OF
ETERNAL SONSHIP

For what saith the scripture?
(Romans 4:3)

God's inerrant Word must be the final authority for all that we believe and teach. Let us prayerfully and carefully search the Scriptures to determine if Jesus Christ became the Son of God at some point in history or if He has eternally existed as the Son of God, basking in the sunlight of the Father's love and enjoying delightful fellowship in the Father's bosom even before the foundation of the world (John 17:5,24; John 1:18).

By the Son all things were created. "Who hath delivered us from the power of darkness, and hath translated us into the kingdom of his dear Son . . . Who is the image of the invisible God . . . by him were all things created . . . And he is before all things, and by him all things consist" (Colossians 1:13-17).

In Colossians 1:13 we learn that we have been translated into the kingdom of the Father's dear Son (literally, "the Son of His love"). The succeeding verses contain a series of pronouns, all of which refer to "his dear Son" in verse 13. W. J. Hocking observed:

We note that all the 15 pronouns in verses 15 to 20 inclusive are in apposition with the noun, Son (v. 13). Each dependent sentence, therefore, declares some fresh glory of the Son, to Whom they all relate, and in Whom they all combine with a transcendent harmony.[1]

Therefore Colossians 1:16 clearly states that by the Son all things were created. All things were created by the Son of His love. The Son of God therefore must have existed as the Son at the time of creation, long before He became incarnate. Those who insist that Christ did not become the Son of God until the incarnation must put a strained interpretation on the clear statement of this verse. A typical explanation from one holding this view would be as follows:

> By the Son all things were created, according to this text, but at the time He did His creative work He was not the Son of God. He was the eternal God, but He did not become the Son of God until His birth thousands of years later. Paul referred to the Creator as the "Son of His love" because we now know Him by this title even though He was not the beloved Son of the Father at the time of creation. Also at the time of creation, the first person of the Trinity was not yet the Father. These were roles that They would assume later. Just as we might refer to the fact that President George Bush played on the baseball team at Yale University even though he was not actually the president when at Yale, so we could say that the Son of God created all things even though He was not the Son of God when He did His creative work.

Such an involved explanation ought to be rejected. We must simply accept the obvious meaning of the text: the

Father created all things by the Son of His love. The normal and natural meaning of this passage is that at the time of creation He existed as the Father's beloved Son.

Hebrews 1:1-2, which is similar to Colossians 1:13-17, also identifies the Creator as the Son of God: "God . . . Hath in these last days spoken unto us by his Son, whom he hath appointed heir of all things, by whom also he made the worlds." It was by the Son that the Father made the worlds. John Darby concluded from this passage that "we are therefore justified in speaking of the Son as before the worlds."[2] Hocking wrote, "Since the Holy Spirit attributes creatorial activity to the Son, His existence must have preceded that of the universe which He called into being."[3] The hymnist declared, "Crown Him the Son of God / Before the worlds began"!

W. E. Vine skillfully showed the bearing of Hebrews 1:2 on the doctrine of eternal Sonship. He pointed out that

> the design in the stress on the word "Son" in verse 2 is not to convey the idea that God has spoken to us in One Who became His Son, but that He has done so in One Whose relationship to Him as Son stands in antecedent existence both to creation and to His incarnation. . . . The passage is itself a testimony to the pre-existent Sonship of Christ; for not only has God spoken to us in Him Who is His Son, but by Him . . . He "made the worlds" (the ages). The plain implication is that He by Whom God made the worlds stood in relationship to Him in this respect as His Son.[4]

The Son of God is the only begotten of the Father. "And we beheld his glory, the glory as of the only begotten of the Father. . . . No man hath seen God at any time; the only begotten Son, which is in the bosom of the Father, he hath declared him" (John 1:14,18).

John beheld the divine glory of the only begotten of the Father, even the unique Son of God. William Hendriksen concluded that John 1:14 must refer to Christ's trinitarian Sonship—that is, "to the fact that He is the Son of God from all eternity." Hendriksen continued: "This is favored by the context (John 1:1,18) and by such passages as 3:16,18, which prove that the Son **was already** the only begotten before his incarnation . . . the sonship here indicated was present **from eternity**" (emphasis his).[5]

J. G. Bellett posed this question for those who teach that Christ was not the Son of God until the incarnation: "Had the Father no bosom till the Babe was born in Bethlehem?" He then answered: "Indeed, fully sure I am, as that inquiry suggests, He had from all eternity. The bosom of the Father was an eternal habitation, enjoyed by the Son, in the ineffable delight of the Father."[6]

Bellett also stated: "Matthew and Mark first notice His Sonship of God at His baptism [Matthew 3:17; Mark 1:11]. Luke goes farther back, and notices it at His birth [Luke 1:35]. But John goes back farther still, even to the immeasurable, unspeakable distance of eternity, and declares His Sonship 'in the bosom of the Father.'"[7]

> Lamb of God, Thy Father's bosom
> Ever was Thy dwelling-place![8]

The Greek construction of John 1:18 is significant with respect to the doctrine of eternal Sonship. The verb translated "which is" can be literally rendered "the One being" or "the One ever existing" in the bosom of the Father. According to Charles Hodge, the Greek construction of this verb expresses permanent being: "He who is, was, and ever shall be, in the bosom of the Father, i.e., most intimately united with Him."[9] W. E. Vine also defended the eternal Sonship of Christ. His comments on John 1:18 are worthy of note:

The plain implication of the pre-existent Sonship of Christ given in verse 14 is confirmed in verse 18 by the description of the Son as the One Who is "in the bosom of the Father." The phraseology employed is that of the definite article with the present participle of the verb "to be," lit., "the (one) being in the bosom . . . " This form of phrase provides what is virtually a titular description, and is to be distinguished from the use of the relative pronoun with the present tense of the verb to be ("who is"). Had it been the intention of the writer to state that the Son is at the present time in the bosom of the Father, in contrast to a time in the past when He was not in that position and relationship, the relative clause, that is to say, the relative pronoun with the present tense, would have been used (i.e., *hos esti*, "who is"). The participial construction (the definite article with the present participle "being") is not thus limited in point of time. Here the construction conveys a time-less description, expressing a condition and relation-ship characteristic, essential and unoriginal.[10]

That He is "the only begotten Son, which is in the bosom of the Father," expresses both His eternal union with the Father in the Godhead, and the ineffable intimacy and love between Them, the Son sharing all the Father's counsels and enjoying all His affections. "The bosom of the Father" ever has been and ever will be the Son's dwelling place.[11]

The unmistakable teaching of John 1:18 is that the Son of God is perfectly qualified to be the revealer of the invisible Father because from all eternity He has existed in the Father's bosom. As Matthew Henry said, "He had lain in his bosom from eternity. . . . In the bosom of his **special love**, dear to him, **in whom he was well pleased**, always his delight" (emphasis his).[12]

God sent His Son. "The Father sent the Son to be the Saviour of the world" (1 John 4:14). "He loved us, and sent his Son" (1 John 4:10). "As my Father hath sent me, even so send I you" (John 20:21). "When the fulness of time was come, God sent forth his Son" (Galatians 4:4).

Numerous verses speak of the Father's sending the Son into this world (just a few of them are cited above). These passages clearly indicate that Jesus was the Son before God sent Him into the world. If God sent His Son, then He must have been the Son even before His mission. "This at least is the most obvious sense of these passages, and the sense which an ordinary reader would doubtless affix to them."[13] The Father sent the One who was already His Son. These verses do not say that God sent forth One who became His Son at the time of His birth.[14] They tell us that prior to His mission He was really and truly related to His Father as Son. J. C. Philpot pointed out the faulty logic of those who teach that the incarnation marked the beginning of Christ's divine Sonship:

> But what unprejudiced mind does not see that sending a person to execute a certain task does not make him to be what he was not before? A master sends a servant to do a certain work; or a father bids a son to perform a certain errand; or a husband desires his wife to execute a certain commission which he has not time or opportunity to do himself; the servant does not cease to be a servant, the son to be a son, nor the wife to be a wife by being so sent.[15]

The wife was a wife before the mission, and she was a wife after the mission. So also the Son of God was the Son of God before His mission (before He came into this world by means of the incarnation) and after the mission.

In Galatians 4:4-6 the term "sent forth" is used in

reference to both the Son and the Spirit. And in John 14:26 the Lord Jesus promised that the Father would "send" the Comforter. Did the third person of the godhead become the Holy Spirit when He was sent or was He already the Holy Spirit prior to His being sent? The answer is obvious. The Holy Spirit did not become the Holy Spirit at Pentecost, just as the Son of God did not become the Son of God at Bethlehem. The Spirit was the Spirit and the Son was the Son prior to Their respective missions. The many verses that speak of God's sending His Son make sense only when we understand that He was the Son prior to His being sent.

The parable of the vineyard owner (Mark 12:1-12) portrays Christ as eternal Son. "Having yet therefore one son, his wellbeloved, he sent him also last unto them, saying, They will reverence my son" (12:6).

It is evident that the son of the vineyard owner was the son before he was sent on his mission. He was his father's son before he was sent. This parable obviously portrays the sending of God's well-beloved Son into a world that rejected and murdered Him. As we reverently ponder this parable, we must conclude that the Lord Jesus was the beloved Son of the Father before He was sent on His mission. Philpot wrote, "If the parable has any force, or indeed any meaning—and it would be sacrilege to say it has not—God the Father must have had a Son in heaven with Him before He sent Him."[16]

God the Father gave His Son. "For God so loved the world, that he gave his only begotten Son" (John 3:16).

How amazing is the love of the Father! What a sacrifice He was willing to make, yielding up the One who was so near and dear to His heart—His well-beloved unique Son who ever was in His bosom! Since God "gave his only begotten Son," Christ was God's Son before He was given. To say that He became God's only begotten Son by the incarnation would rob John 3:16 of its meaning, force, and preciousness. Vine wrote: "The value and greatness of the gift lay in the Sonship of Him who was given. His Sonship was not the effect of His being given."[17] Philpot reasoned:

> Now must He not have existed as His Son before He gave Him? If I give a person a thing, my giving it does not change the nature of the object given, does not make it different from what it was before I gave it. So, if God so loved the world as to give His only-begotten Son, He must surely have been His only-begotten Son before He gave Him. . . . His giving Him could not make Him His only-begotten Son, because the wondrous love consisted in this, that though He was God's only-begotten Son, still He gave Him. Any other interpretation quite destroys the meaning and force of the passage.[18]

Hocking agreed:

> The measure of God's love of the world is to be seen in His giving the One Who was peculiarly and exclusively the object of His affection—His Only-begotten Son. The stupendous wonder to our faith is that One was along with God in this unique relationship of Son, and God gave that One. This is surely the teaching of the text, not that God's gift was One Who became His Only-begotten Son in manhood, that is, in the process and at the time of giving. If Sonship began in incarnation, why do we not read that God gave the Son of man? But no, the Only-begotten Son of God was given. . . . To think otherwise of Him than as the Eternal Son is to detract from the personal glory of God's incomparable gift.[19]

Romans 8:32 asks, "He that spared not his own Son, but delivered him up for us all, how shall he not with him also freely give us all things?" This verse reminds us of the time when Abraham delivered up his son Isaac (Genesis 22). The patriarch was told to take his only son, whom he loved, and bring him to an altar of sacrifice. Surely Isaac, who was a type of Christ (Hebrews 11:19), was Abraham's son long before he was delivered up to the altar. It was the loving father/son relationship already existing that made this sacrifice so costly. God the Father took His Son—His unique Son Jesus, the One whom He loved before the foundation of the world—and delivered Him up for us all. Love so amazing!

If God had spared His Son (and we shudder even to think about this), then there would be no Savior for sinners. We would be without hope and without help. If the Father had not sent His Son, had not given His Son, salvation would have been impossible. But He still would have been the Son of God, because this is who He is, essentially and inherently. He is truly and properly the Son of God because of His eternal relationship to the Father, not because of His incarnate mission. His saviorhood relates to His incarnate mission (Matthew 1:21; John 3:17), but His Sonship relates to His eternal person. Thanks be to God that the Son was sent and was given for our sakes—the One who was with the Father from the very beginning (John 1:1-2; 1 John 1:1-2).

Long ago the prophet Isaiah proclaimed this message: "Unto us a child is born, unto us a son is given" (Isaiah 9:6). As to His humanity, the Lord Jesus was the child who was born. As to His deity, He was the Son who was given by the Father (compare John 3:16). Christ became a child, but He did not become the Son. He who was God's Son from all eternity was sent forth on a saving mission and was "made of a woman" nearly two thousand years ago (Galatians 4:4). His divine Sonship did not come about by human birth.

Christ had a relationship with the Father prior to the incarnation. "I came forth from the Father, and am come into the world: again, I leave the world, and go to the Father" (John 16:28).

How could He come forth from the Father if His existence as the Son did not begin until the incarnation? John 16:28 clearly implies that He was with the Father before coming into the world and thus there must have existed a Father/Son relationship prior to Bethlehem. If Christ did not become the Son until the incarnation, we might expect this verse to say something like this: "I came forth from God and then I became the Son. I leave the world and go back to God who ever since My birth has been My Father." Vine wrote:

> His return to the Father was in the reverse order of procedure to that of His coming. He came from Heaven to the world; He returned from the world to Heaven. He speaks of the One from Whom He came as "the Father," not in the sense that He came out from One Who subsequently became the Father at His birth, but from One Who was the Father when He came out.[20]

We enter holy ground as we listen to the Son praying to His Father: "And now, O Father, glorify thou me with thine own self with the glory which I had with thee before the world was. . . . thou lovedst me before the foundation of the world" (John 17:5,24). These verses bring us back to the time prior to creation. Before the world ever was, the Father and the Son existed in an intimate, loving relationship. People who believe that Christ was not the Son until the incarnation must interpret these verses differently. They say that before the foundation of the world, the Father was not yet the Father and the Son was not yet the Son; the

Father and the Son were nameless persons of the Trinity who would not assume their Father/Son roles until the incarnation. Such an understanding is forced, irreverent, and out of harmony with the clear, simple statements of Scripture. Vine wisely asked, "If that pre-existent love was not between the Father and the Son, what could have been the relationship in which it was exercised?"[21]

In 1 John 1:1-2 we learn that the Word was in the beginning and the Word was with the Father. If Jesus was with the Father from the beginning, He must have been there as the Father's Son. Vine wrote: "The term 'Father' implies the existence of a Son. . . . He does not here say that He who was the Life was 'with God,' but that He was 'with the Father.'"[22] Because the Father/Son relationship existed from the very beginning, Jesus must be the eternal Son.

The Son of God became the Son of David. "Concerning his Son Jesus Christ our Lord, which was made of the seed of David according to the flesh; And declared to be the Son of God with power, according to the spirit of holiness, by the resurrection from the dead" (Romans 1:3-4).

He was David's Son from Bethlehem; He was God's Son from all eternity. He became the Son of David by human birth, but He did not become the Son of God. Benjamin Warfield said it well:

> He who always was and continues to be the Son of God was manifested to men first as the Son of David, and then, after His resurrection, as also the exalted Lord. He always was in the essence of His being the Son of God; this Son of God became of the seed of David and was installed as—what He always was— the Son of God, though now in His proper power, by the resurrection of the dead.[23]

It is helpful to compare Romans 1 to John 1. John wrote, "The Word was made flesh" (John 1:14). Paul also spoke of the incarnation when he wrote that the Son "was made of the seed of David" (Romans 1:3). Christ existed as the Word long before He became flesh (John 1:1-2). Likewise He existed as the Son long before He became David's seed according to the flesh. John 1 tells us that He who was God became flesh. Romans 1 tell us that He who was the Son of God became the Son of David. At the incarnation the eternal God became flesh and the eternal Son became a man. The eternal God did not become the Son. On the contrary "we believe that the Lord Jesus Christ, the eternal Son of God, became man, without ceasing to be God."[24]

His Sonship had no beginning but it did have a manifestation. "For this purpose the Son of God was manifested, that he might destroy the works of the devil" (1 John 3:8).

It is one thing to speak of the manifestation of the Son of God.[25] This is Biblical. It is quite another thing to speak of the origination of the Son of God. This is heretical. His Sonship had no beginning. The verb *to make manifest* means "to make visible or to bring to light what has previously been hidden." Hocking wrote:

> The idea of manifestation is never a transition from a state of non-existence to that of existence. . . . Accordingly, if we would do the honour to the Son that is due Him, we must acknowledge that He was the Son of God before His manifestation. . . . Being Son of God eternally, He has been manifested publicly and visibly in flesh for His mediatorial work."[26]

Melchizedek was a type of the eternal Son of God. "Without father, without mother, without descent, having neither beginning of days, nor end of life; but made like unto the Son of God; abideth a priest continually" (Hebrews 7:3).

The strong testimony that this verse presents for the eternal Sonship of Christ must not be missed. The blessed Spirit of God guided the pen of Moses in such a way that the biography of Melchizedek says nothing about his parents or his birth or his age or his death. These deliberate omissions were for the purpose of presenting Melchizedek as a type of the Son of God: "He was made 'like unto the Son of God,' and the similarity lay in this, that he had 'neither beginning of days nor end of life.' Accordingly it was as the Son of God that Christ was without beginning of days. His Sonship was therefore unoriginated and eternal."[27] As the "Son of God" He was "without father, without mother, without descent, having neither beginning of days, nor end of life."

Those who hold the view that *Son of God* is an incarnate title or role would falsify this verse because in His incarnation as the Son of man the Lord Jesus did have a mother (Galatians 4:4), did have a descent or genealogy (Matthew 1 and Luke 3), did have a beginning of days (compare Luke 3:23), and did have an end of life (He died). However, His divine Sonship has nothing to do with human parents, human lineage, human birth, or time measurements; it is an eternal Sonship.

May the reader thoughtfully consider the united testimony of the many passages cited in this chapter and form safe and solid conclusions based upon "Thus saith the Lord!" May we search the Scriptures diligently and daily to see if these things be so.

Chapter 7

THE MEANING OF THE TERM "SON OF GOD"

And I saw, and bear record that this is the Son of God (John 1:34).

The term *son* has a threefold significance. It signifies that a son is a separate person from his father; a son is the heir, not the servant, of his father; and a son has the same nature as his father. Let's develop and apply these three points to the vitally important issue of the Sonship of Christ.

A son is a separate person from his father.

The fact that a son is a separate person from his father is self-evident. In light of this, Jesus' designation as the Son of God signifies that He is a separate person from God the Father. Various statements Jesus made concerning His relationship with the Father emphasize this truth. For example in John 5:19-22 He said:

> The Son can do nothing of himself, but what he seeth the Father do: for what things soever he doeth, these also doeth the Son likewise. For the Father loveth the Son, and sheweth him all things that himself doeth: and he will shew him greater works than these, that ye may marvel. For as the Father

raiseth up the dead, and quickeneth them; even so the Son quickeneth whom he will. For the Father judgeth no man, but hath committed all judgment unto the Son.

In John 6:38-39 Jesus declared:

For I came down from heaven, not to do mine own will, but the will of him that sent me. And this is the Father's will which hath sent me, that of all which he hath given me I should lose nothing, but should raise it up again at the last day.

These statements can only make sense if Jesus as the Son is a separate person from the Father.

A son is the heir, not the servant, of his father.

The term *son* signifies that a son is not a servant of his father. In contrast to his father's servants, a son is his father's heir. Scripture illustrates this contrast between a servant and a son in several ways.

First, the Lord Jesus contrasted servant and son in the parable of a householder who planted a vineyard and turned it over to the care of husbandmen (Matthew 21:33-39). When the harvest season came, the householder sent servants to the vineyard to collect his share of the harvest. The husbandmen abused and killed the servants. Since the husbandmen did not respect his servants, the householder finally decided to send his son. He said, "They will reverence my son" (21:37). The householder's decision and statement indicate a clear distinction in his mind between his servants and his son.

When the son arrived at the vineyard, the husbandmen said, "This is the heir; come, let us kill him, and let us seize on his inheritance" (Matthew 21:38). This statement indicates that a son (not the servants) is his father's heir.

In this parable the householder represents God the Father; the householder's servants represent God's Old Testament prophets; and the householder's son represents Christ, the Son of God. Through this parable Jesus drew a contrast between God's servants (the prophets) and Himself as God's Son and heir.

Second, in the parable of the prodigal son (Luke 15:11-32) Jesus contrasted servant and son. When the prodigal son came to his senses and decided to return home, he determined to say to his father, "I . . . am no more worthy to be called thy son: make me as one of thy hired servants" (15:18-19). When the son returned, the father ordered his servants to do beneficial things for his son (15:22-24). The elder son called one of the servants and asked him for information (15:25-26). All of these details in the story indicate a contrast between a servant and a son.

Third, Paul contrasted servant and son: "Wherefore thou art no more a servant, but a son; and if a son, then an heir of God through Christ" (Galatians 4:7).

Fourth, to demonstrate the superiority of Christ over Moses, Scripture presents Moses as a servant of God in contrast to Christ who is the Son and heir of God (Hebrews 3:5-6). Concerning this contrast F. F. Bruce wrote:

> Moses' relation to God's household, then, was that of a servant; Christ's relation to it is that of the Son and heir. Moses served *in* the household as one who was himself part of the household; Christ rules *over* the household as the Son whom His Father, the owner of the household, has appointed to exercise this rule. The Son's authority is greater than the servant's.[1]

Hebrews also presents Christ as being superior to the angels. Christ is set forth as Son (1:2,5-6,8) and heir (1:2,4), whereas the angels are called ministers or servants (1:7,14).

In light of these contrasts between a servant and a son, we can conclude that subservience to one's father is not associated with the Biblical idea of sonship. Christ as Son is the Father's heir, not His servant.

A son has the same nature as his father.

The term *son* also signifies that a son has the same nature as his father. In the Old Testament and in the writings of post-Biblical Judaism, the Hebrew words for *son* were "often used to denote the relationship which determines the nature of a man."[2] Thus Jesus' designation as the Son of God indicates that He has the same nature as the Father. He is as fully divine as the Father.

The Scriptures give evidence supporting the conclusion that the term *the Son of God* signifies the divine nature of Jesus. Let's look at nine of these Scriptural proofs.

First, the Bible makes it clear that the Jews recognized that absolute deity is inherent in the expression *the Son of God.* Because Jesus called God "My Father" the Jews "sought the more to kill him, because he not only had broken the sabbath, but said also that God was his Father, making himself equal with God" (John 5:17-18). On another occasion as Jews attempted to kill Jesus they said, "For a good work we stone thee not; but for blasphemy; and because that thou, being a man, makest thyself God" (John 10:33). Replying to this charge Jesus asked, "Say ye of him, whom the Father hath sanctified, and sent into the world, Thou blasphemest; because I said, I am the Son of God?" (John 10:36). This reply indicates that it was His claim to be the Son of God that prompted the Jews to accuse Him of making Himself God. A comparison of Matthew 26:63-66 and Luke 22:66-71 further substantiates that the religious rulers of Israel accused Jesus of blasphemy because He claimed to be the Son of God.

Second, in Hebrews 1 the Father ascribes deity to Jesus as the Son of God. "But unto the Son he saith, Thy throne, O God, is for ever and ever" (1:8). "Therefore God, even thy God, hath anointed thee with the oil of gladness above thy fellows" (1:9). In both statements the Father calls His Son *God.*

Third, Scripture refers to the incarnated Christ as both the Son of God and the Son of man. What would be the purpose of these two designations, except to emphasize His two natures—human and divine? One language scholar stated that the expression *Son of man* "denotes true humanity."[3] Another scholar declared that it clearly "signifies what essentially appertains to man, to human nature in its inner reality."[4] Another asserted that "it refers to Christ's humanity. . . . It therefore stresses His manhood . . . partaking of the characteristics (sin apart) of manhood belonging to the category of mankind."[5]

If the expression *the Son of man* indicates Christ's humanity, then the expression *the Son of God* must indicate His deity. Another language scholar wrote, "Unquestionably the title 'Son of God' affirms the full deity of Jesus, as the title 'Son of Man' affirms his true humanity."[6]

Fourth, in John 10:30 Jesus claimed to be one with the Father. The fact that Jesus called God *Father* indicates that He was speaking as God's Son. As God's Son, He was claiming to be one in nature with the Father.

Fifth, in John 5:19-21,25-26 Jesus as Son claimed to have equal authority or power with the Father. Jesus asserted that He does the same things as the Father. He and the Father both raise the dead; He and the Father both have life in themselves.

Sixth, in John 5:23 Jesus as Son claimed to have equal honor with the Father: "All men should honour the Son, even as they honour the Father. He that honoureth not the Son honoureth not the Father which hath sent him."

Seventh, Hebrews 1:2 reveals that God made the worlds by His Son. According to this declaration the Son of God is the Creator. Only deity can be the Creator.

THE ETERNAL SONSHIP OF CHRIST

Eighth, Hebrews 1:2-3 asserts that as the Son of God, Jesus is the brightness of God's glory, thus identifying the Son with the shekinah glory of God. The shekinah glory always signified the presence of deity, so the identification of the Son with the shekinah glory is an identification of the Son with deity. When Jesus displayed the shekinah glory in His person at His transfiguration, the Father clearly acknowledged Him to be His Son (Matthew 17:1-5).

Hebrews 1:2-3 also states that as the Son of God Jesus is "the express image of [God's] person." The Greek word that is translated *express image* means "impress, reproduction, exact representation."[7] Judaism used this term to refer to "the likeness between parents and children."[8] The Greek word that is translated *person* means "substantial nature, essence, actual being, reality."[9] With these definitions in mind, one language scholar concluded that Hebrews 1:2-3 presents the concept that "Christ as the Son of God is the impress of God's nature."[10]

Ninth, the Scriptural expression *the only begotten Son* indicates that the designation *the Son of God* signifies the divine nature of Jesus. In contrast to believers who are begotten of God (John 1:13; 1 John 3:9; 4:7; 5:1,4,18) and are sons of God (Romans 8:14; Galatians 3:26), Christ is "the only begotten Son" of God (John 3:16,18; 1 John 4:9). Christ is the Son of God in a way that believers are not. He is uniquely the Son of God. John, who alone used the term *only begotten* to describe Christ, used it to emphasize "more strongly the distinction between Jesus and believers and the uniqueness of Jesus in His divine sonship."[11]

Jesus emphasized the concept of His unique Sonship when He declared "that God was his Father" (John 5:18). The Greek word that is translated *his* in this verse literally means "his own," "in contrast to what is public property or belongs to another."[12] The Jews recognized that Christ, through this declaration, was "making himself equal with God."

Christ is related to the divine nature in a way that believers are not. As begotten of God and sons of God believers are partakers of the holiness aspect of God's divine nature (2 Peter 1:4), but not His other attributes. As the only begotten Son of God, Christ possesses the total nature of God.

Angels are called "the sons of God" (Job 2:1); God referred to the nation Israel and to King Solomon as "my son" (Exodus 4:22; 2 Samuel 7:14); and Adam is designated "the son of God" (Luke 3:38). But Christ alone is called the only begotten Son of God. Others are called God's sons to indicate that God brought them into existence or installed them in their positions. Christ is designated the only begotten Son of God because He possesses the same divine nature as God and has a unique eternal relationship with the Father.

We can conclude that the expression *the Son of God* indicates absolute deity for Jesus Christ. As the Son He has the same nature as the Father and is a separate person from the Father. One scholar said, "The title has already become a cipher which presupposes a unity of essence between Father and Son."[13] Another wrote, "Thus, absolute Godhead, not Godhead in a secondary or derived sense, is intended in the title."[14]

Since the expression *the Son of God* indicates absolute deity and since Christ has always been deity, we can conclude that Christ has always been the Son of God and we can rule out the idea that Christ *became* the Son of God at some point in history. A person who claims that Christ became the Son of God either at His conception, birth, baptism, or resurrection and therefore was not the Son of God before His incarnation, should also deny the preincarnate deity of Christ in order to be consistent.

Chapter 8

THE MEANING OF PSALM 2:7

"I will declare the decree: the Lord hath said unto me, Thou art my Son; this day have I begotten thee" (Psalm 2:7). Jesus Christ was "declared to be the Son of God with power, according to the spirit of holiness, by the resurrection from the dead" (Romans 1:4).

P salm 2 begins on a tumultuous note. Verses 1-3 describe world conditions when the Messiah returns to earth to establish the millennial kingdom and administer God's rule worldwide. With grim determination Gentile rulers and their armies will unite to try to prevent the establishment of divine Messianic rule (cf. Revelation 16:12-16; 19:11-21). God will laugh at the puniness of this stubborn rebellious opposition to His omnipotent power, will pour out His wrath on the rebels, and will establish His Messiah as King in spite of the Gentiles' resistance (Psalm 2:4-6).

Verse 7 begins to relate what the Messiah will say when He returns in His second coming. At the time Messiah takes over the rule of the earth He will declare what God had already decreed concerning Him: "Thou art my Son; this day have I begotten thee." How does this Psalm 2:7 statement relate to the eternal Sonship of Jesus Christ? Does the statement indicate that Christ *became* the Son of God at some point in history (on the day that God begot Him) and therefore is not eternally the Son of God? To answer these questions we must examine Paul's use of the Psalm 2:7 statement in Acts 13:33.

Having talked about God's promise to give Israel a Savior from David's lineage, Paul made the following declaration in Acts 13:33: "God hath fulfilled the same unto us their children, in that he hath raised up Jesus again; as it is also written in the second psalm, Thou art my Son, this day have I begotten thee." This verse indicates that God's raising up of Jesus fulfilled His Psalm 2:7 decree concerning the Messiah. Paul seemed to be saying that God begot the Messiah as His Son when He raised up Jesus. What did Paul mean when he said that God "hath raised up Jesus"?

Two interpretations of Paul's declaration

Many interpreters believe that Paul had the following meaning in mind: God raised up Jesus to deliver Israel from its oppressors in the same sense that He raised up Moses to deliver Israel from its Egyptian oppressors. God raised up Jesus by sending Him into the world incarnated in human flesh to be the deliverer. The raising up took place at Christ's incarnation, the day that God begot His humanity. Some who believe this interpretation conclude that since the raising up of Jesus fulfilled God's Psalm 2:7 decree concerning the Messiah and took place at Christ's incarnation, Christ *became* the Son of God at the time of His incarnation.

There is a major problem with this conclusion. In chapter 7 we noted that the expression *the Son of God* indicates absolute deity for Jesus Christ and the expression *the Son of man* indicates His humanity. Since God begot Christ's humanity, not His deity, at the time of the incarnation, it follows that Christ became the Son of man, not the Son of God, at the time of His incarnation.

Other scholars propose a different interpretation of Paul's statement concerning the raising up of Jesus. They believe that Paul was referring to the bodily resurrection of Christ. According to this interpretation God's Psalm 2:7 decree concerning the Messiah was fulfilled when Jesus rose from the dead. This would mean that Paul was linking Christ's resurrection, His being the promised deliverer, and His being the Son of God.

The reason for favoring the resurrection interpretation

I favor the resurrection interpretation for the following reason: The context (Acts 13:23,32) of Paul's statement indicates that in Acts 13:33 he was saying that the raising up of Jesus fulfilled God's promise to give Israel a deliverer from David's lineage, and a parallel passage (Paul's defense before Agrippa in Acts 26) makes it clear that hope for the fulfillment of God's promise was dependent on resurrection from the dead—specifically Christ's resurrection from the dead.

> And now I stand and am judged for the hope of the promise made of God unto our fathers: Unto which promise our twelve tribes, instantly serving God day and night, hope to come. For which hope's sake, king Agrippa, I am accused of the Jews. Why should it be thought a thing incredible with you, that God should raise the dead? (Acts 26:6-8)

> Having therefore obtained help of God, I continue unto this day, witnessing both to small and great, saying none other things than those which the prophets and Moses did say should come: That Christ should suffer, and that he should be the first that should rise from the dead, and should shew light unto the people, and to the Gentiles (Acts 26:22-23).

F. F. Bruce made the following comments concerning Paul's statements in Acts 26:

> That a faithful Pharisee believed in the resurrection of the dead, and saw no fulfillment of Israel's

ancient hope apart from the resurrection, went
without saying. But the amazing and indeed absurd
feature of the present dispute was that he was being
prosecuted for his proclamation of this very hope—
and prosecuted by Jews, of all people! But this hope
was the hope that God would keep the promise
which He made to the fathers of the nation long ago;
it was the hope which gave life and meaning and
purpose to the ordinance of divine worship, faithfully maintained by all twelve tribes of Israel generation after generation—the hope that God would
one day come down to deliver His people as He had
done when they were slaves in Egypt, that He would
raise up a horn of salvation for them "in the house
of His servant David, as He spoke by the mouth of
His holy prophets from of old" (cf. Luke 1:69f.).
Why should they think it incredible that God should
raise the dead? The Pharisees would answer that
they did not think it incredible; they ardently believed in God as the raiser of the dead. But Paul's
point was that this belief had now been validated in
that God had already raised up one man from the
dead, and had by that very fact demonstrated that
man to be Israel's long-expected Messiah and Deliverer, the one in whom the age-old hope was real-
ized. Why should those who believed in the resurrection of the dead refuse to believe that God had in
fact raised up Jesus, and so declared Him to be the
Son of God?[1]

Since Paul's statements in Acts 26 are parallel to his
Acts 13 statement and make it clear that the fulfillment of
God's promise to the Israelite fathers was dependent on
Christ's resurrection from the dead, it would appear that
the Acts 13:33 reference to God's raising up of Jesus
concerns His bodily resurrection from the dead.

The resurrection interpretation leads to the following conclusions: God's Psalm 2:7 decree concerning the Messiah was fulfilled when Jesus rose from the dead; there is a sense in which God begot Christ on His resurrection day; and there is a sense in which Christ's being the Son of God is related to His resurrection.

In what sense did God beget Christ on His resurrection day?

It should be noted that the Hebrew word that is translated "begotten" in Psalm 2:7 does not always mean "beget" in the sense of conception. Its more frequent meaning is to "bear, bring forth" in the sense of giving birth (1 Kings 3:17-18; 2 Kings 19:3).[2] Just as a baby is hidden from sight in his mother's womb until he is brought forth on the day of his birth, so Christ after His death was hidden from sight in the womb of the earth until God brought Him forth on the day of His resurrection. Thus on Christ's resurrection day God begot Him in the sense of bringing Him forth alive from the grave.

We should note that the Hebrew Old Testament presented the concept of Hades as being a womb.[3] The Septuagint (the Greek translation of the Old Testament) also used verbs "which describe how the womb of death or Hades gives up those who are kept in it . . . The pangs of death and Hades are the presupposition of birth from death and its kingdom."[4] Ancient Judaism associated the idea of birth with resurrection from the dead. In 4 Esdras 4:42 "the comparison with a woman in childbirth serves to represent new birth in the resurrection. Sheol and the chambers of souls are like the womb which after a certain time can no longer hold the child."[5] In the rabbinic tradition "most Rabb. adopt the metaphor of the womb of the earth and hence of labour and its pangs."[6]

Peter in his Pentecost message associated the idea of birth with Christ's resurrection when he declared, "Whom God hath raised up, having loosed the pains [literally, birth

pangs] of death: because it was not possible that he should
be holden of it" (Acts 2:24). Concerning Peter's declaration
Georg Bertram wrote:

> In Acts 2:24 the ref. is to the birth of Messiah or
> rather to new birth through the resurrection . . . God
> Himself has relieved the pangs of birth out of death.
> The abyss can no more hold the Redeemer than a
> pregnant woman can hold the child in her body.
> Under severe labour pains the womb of the under-
> world must release the Redeemer. God Himself helps
> it to end the pains.[7]

In what sense is Christ's being the Son of God related to His resurrection?

Historical background sheds light on this issue. In the
ancient Roman empire crucifixion was regarded as the
most cruel, disgusting, and shameful form of death ever
devised.[8] Cicero, Roman orator and writer (106-43 B.C.),
described it as "that most cruel and disgusting penalty."[9]
On another occasion he said that "the very word 'cross'
should be far removed not only from the person of a Roman
citizen but from his thoughts, his eyes and his ears."[10]
Josephus, famous Jewish historian (A.D. 37-95), called crucifixion "the most wretched of deaths."[11] Ancients classified death on a cross as the supreme Roman penalty, even
worse than burning and decapitation.[12]

Because crucifixion was so horrible the ancient world
believed that only rebellious foreigners, violent criminals
and robbers, and slaves deserved to die that form of death.[13]
Therefore any person who died on a cross was automatically classified as a rebel, criminal, or slave. Thus both Jews
and Gentiles were convinced that it would be impossible
for the Son of God to be crucified.[14]

To the Gentile way of thinking, since the gods of
Greece and Rome were immortal (in contrast to mortal

men), it would be impossible for them to die on a cross.[15] Celsus, a vocal pagan opponent of early Christianity, said, "But if he [Jesus] was really so great he ought, in order to display his divinity, to have disappeared suddenly from the cross."[16] Thus the Greeks and Romans automatically rejected any claim to divine Sonship by anyone who died on a cross. Martin Hengel wrote:

> To believe that the one pre-existent Son of the one true God, the mediator at creation and the redeemer of the world, had appeared in very recent times in out-of-the-way Galilee as a member of the obscure people of the Jews, and even worse, had died the death of a common criminal on the cross, could only be regarded as a sign of madness.[17]

On the basis of Deuteronomy 21:23 ("He that is hanged is accursed of God") the Jews concluded that to be hanged on a cross is to be cursed of God, and certainly God, if He had a Son, would never curse His own Son.[18] The fact that the Jews were convinced that no Son of God could die by crucifixion is evidenced by the abuse they hurled at Jesus while He was on the cross:

> And they that passed by reviled him, wagging their heads, And saying, Thou that destroyest the temple, and buildest it in three days, save thyself. If thou be the Son of God, come down from the cross. Likewise also the chief priests mocking him, with the scribes and elders, said, He saved others; himself he cannot save. If he be the King of Israel, let him now come down from the cross, and we will believe him. He trusted in God; let him deliver him now, if he will have him: for he said, I am the Son of God. The thieves also, which were crucified with him, cast the same in his teeth (Matthew 27:39-44).

Israel rejected Jesus' claim to be the Son of God and the Messiah (Matthew 26:63-66; Acts 13:27-29). His death by crucifixion convinced the Jews that their rejection of Him was correct.

How does this historical background shed light on the sense in which Christ's being the Son of God is related to His resurrection? God's resurrecting of Jesus was His way of decreeing to the world that in spite of His crucifixion Jesus is the Son of God, the One uniquely qualified to be God's representative ruler for the millennium. In Acts 17:31 Paul declared that by raising Jesus from the dead God gave proof to all men that Jesus is the man whom He has ordained to have authority over the world. After pointing out that Jesus Christ, God's Son, "was made of the seed of David according to the flesh" Paul asserted that He was "declared to be the Son of God with power, according to the spirit of holiness, by the resurrection from the dead" (Romans 1:3-4; cf. Acts 13:22-23,30-33). In other words, on the day of Jesus' resurrection God showed Israel to be wrong in their conclusion that Jesus Christ was not the Son of God, the One uniquely qualified to be the Messiah, the nation's deliverer.

The results of our examination of the relationship of Psalm 2:7 to Acts 13:33 lead us to the following understanding: In Acts 13:33 Paul indicated that God's resurrecting of Jesus fulfilled His Psalm 2:7 decree concerning the Messiah. The day that God raised Jesus from the dead He begot Him as His Son in the sense that He brought Jesus forth from the womb of the earth by resurrection and thereby publicly decreed Him to be His Son. God did not beget Jesus in the sense of conceiving or making Him the divine Son on His resurrection day. (Jesus was already the Son of God before His resurrection, as recorded in Matthew 3:16-17; 17:1-5.)

This understanding of the Psalm 2:7 decree has great significance for the rest of Psalm 2. As noted earlier, Psalm 2 foretells world conditions when Messiah returns to earth to establish the millennial kingdom and administer God's rule worldwide. Gentile rulers and armies will unite to try to prevent the establishment of divine Messianic rule. Psalm 2:7 foretells that at that time Messiah will declare what God decreed concerning Him by resurrecting Him from the dead (He is the Son of God, the One having the same divine nature as the Father, and therefore the One uniquely qualified to be God's representative ruler). This declaring of God's decree will be Jesus' way of asserting that He is the legitimate ruler of the world who has the right and authority to take over the earth.

To summarize, Psalm 2:7 does not militate against the eternal Sonship of Jesus Christ. It does not refer to a time when Christ *became* the Son of God through a begetting act of God. Instead it refers to the day of Jesus' resurrection when God brought Him forth from the womb of the earth and thereby publicly decreed that He is who He always was—the Son of God.

Chapter 9

DEALING WITH PROBLEMS AND OBJECTIONS

Jesus answered and said unto them, Ye do err, not
knowing the scriptures, nor the power of God
(Matthew 22:29).

S tones are being hurled at the impregnable fortress known as the doctrine of eternal Sonship. Objections are being raised against this cherished precious truth that concerns the second person of the triune God and His relationship to the Father. We should not be surprised that the Bible's true teaching regarding the person of the Son is under attack. The essence of Christianity revolves around Jesus Christ and who He really is. Believers need to be extremely careful to remain and abide in the true doctrine of Christ (2 John 9).

No Biblical doctrine is without its problems. Countless objections have been raised against vital doctrines of the faith such as the deity of Christ, the Trinity, the substitutionary atonement, eternal punishment, and the second coming of Christ. Our frail feeble minds have difficulty grasping the depths and wonders of God's revelation. Our thoughts are not His thoughts, and only humble submission to the written Word of God as taught by the blessed Spirit of God will enable us to correct our thinking and bring it more into harmony with God's truth. Trusting

God to be our infallible teacher and looking to God's Word as our inerrant guide, let us now deal with some objections and problems relating to eternal Sonship.

Second Samuel 7:14 indicates that His Sonship is yet future: "I will be his father, and he shall be my son."

Opponents of eternal Sonship sometimes emphasize the future tense in this verse: "I will . . . he shall." They argue that when God gave this promise, the second person of the Trinity was not yet the Son of God but that He would become the Son at the incarnation. Likewise they insist that the first person of the Trinity did not become the Father until Christ was born. They deny the eternal Sonship of the second person and they deny the eternal fatherhood of the first person. While they rightly understand the promise to mean that the future King would be the Son of God, they err in their unwarranted conclusion that prior to the incarnation Christ did not exist as the beloved and eternal Son of the Father. According to Christ's divine nature He was the Son of God from all eternity (Romans 1:3-4).[1]

What is in view in 2 Samuel 7:14 is not Christ's relationship in the godhead as the preincarnate Son of God, but His relationship to the Father as the Son of David. The emphasis is on relationship, not origin. The Davidic covenant (2 Samuel 7:4-17 and 1 Chronicles 17:3-15) emphasizes the humanity of Christ. He was the human Son and descendant of David, the rightful heir to the throne (Luke 1:32-33). The man Christ Jesus, the promised Messiah, would have a special Father/Son relationship with God. The Messiah, God's Son, would be a man possessing and exhibiting the same nature as God.

William R. Newell, a firm defender of the doctrine of eternal Sonship, commented on 2 Samuel 7:14 as it is quoted in Hebrews 1:5: "I will be to him a Father, and he shall be to me a Son." Newell wrote:

How wonderfully the Spirit of God brings out the thought of God, where our poor minds could not have followed! The words, **He shall be to Me a Son**, are of course spoken of Christ as a Son of David—as Man. As God He was eternally in the relationship of Son. Again we would warn against seeking to probe into this mystery, which faith and faith alone can receive. A godly and deeply instructed brother has written: "We cannot fathom what He was. Our hearts should not go and scrutinize the Person of Christ as though we could know it all. No human being can understand the union of God and man in His Person: 'No one knoweth the Son, save the Father' . . . All that is revealed, you may know; we may learn a great deal about Him . . . but when I attempt to fathom the union of God and man . . . no man can."[2]

Those who teach that the Son did not become the Son and the Father did not become the Father until the incarnation face a problem. In the opening chapter of the Bible we are told that "the Spirit of God moved upon the face of the waters" (Genesis 1:2). The third person of the Trinity is clearly identified in this verse as being the Spirit of God at the time of creation. Are we to believe that the third person of the Trinity assumed His "role" as the Spirit thousands of years before the Father became the Father and the Son became the Son? No, He is eternally the Spirit. Indeed He is called "the eternal Spirit" (Hebrews 9:14). Likewise the Son is eternally the Son, and at the time of creation the Father made all things by the Son (Colossians 1:13,16). The Father, Son, and Holy Spirit were all actively involved in the great work of creation. May the name of the triune God be forever praised!

Luke 1:35 indicates that Christ's Sonship began at His birth: "And the angel answered and said unto her, The

Holy Ghost shall come upon thee, and the power of the Highest shall overshadow thee: therefore also that holy thing which shall be born of thee shall be called the Son of God."

Those who teach that our Lord's Sonship began at the incarnation frequently use this verse as a proof text. We should be careful to notice, however, that the passage does not say that He would *become* the Son of God, but that He should be *called* the Son of God. At His birth the Messiah would be called the Son of God because that is exactly who He was. He became the Son of man—the Son of David—at birth (Romans 1:3-4). He did not become the Son of God at birth. His humanity had a beginning because He was not always a man. His deity has no beginning because He has always been God. His relationship with the Father cannot be dated. It is eternal.

Luke 1:35 does not mark the beginning of Christ's Sonship. It does, however, mark the beginning of something important. For the first time in history a baby was called the Son of God. For the first time in history a man born of a woman was called "the Son of the Highest" (Luke 1:32). The glory of the incarnation is that He who eternally existed as the Son of God stooped to become a man without ceasing to be God.[3] The incarnate One is clearly identified as God's unique Son (Luke 1:32,35). The God-Man possesses and exhibits the same nature as the Father.

The One who was born in Bethlehem was the Son who "came forth from the Father" (John 16:28) and had been "sent forth" by the Father (Galatians 4:4). According to Isaiah 9:6 the child who would be born would be called the "mighty God." Obviously He existed as the mighty God long before He was called this, just as He existed as the Son of God long before the angel announced that He would be called the Son at His birth. His Sonship did not originate through conception in Nazareth or through birth in

Bethlehem. At the baptism and the transfiguration, God clearly identified His Son. At His birth Christ was clearly identified as the Son of God as well.[4]

In the Old Testament Christ is never called God's Son except prophetically.

Some people believe that the references to God's Son in Psalm 2 are prophetic. When this Psalm was written, they say, Christ was not the Son of God—the prophecy points toward a future day when He would indeed be the Son of God, beginning with His incarnation.

In Psalm 2:12 the kings of the earth are told to "kiss the Son, lest he be angry." A blessing is pronounced upon all kings and rulers who put their trust in God's Son. This verse is in sharp contrast to the future scene, introduced prophetically in Psalm 2:2, when all the kings of the earth will be gathered together against Jehovah and against His Son the Messiah. In that day the Christ-hating rulers of the earth will not kiss the Son. Any king reading this Psalm even during Old Testament times could say, "I do not want to be like those future kings who will declare their independence from God. Instead I want to kiss the Son and honor Him and trust in a great God who can bless my heart." The reference to God's Son in Psalm 2:2-9 is definitely prophetic; these verses describe the time just prior to Messiah's second coming to earth. Psalm 2:10-12 is the personal application of the prophecy and the reference to God's Son there is not prophetic. Any king or ruler or judge reading this Psalm could apply those verses to Himself and realize that he has a responsibility to trust in God's Son the Messiah.

Those who do not believe that Christ is the eternal Son also say that Isaiah 9:6 is prophetic. This verse speaks of the time when God's Son would be given. However, the fact that God gave His Son implies that He existed as the Son before He was given. The greatness of God's gift lay in the fact that He gave One who is eternally His beloved Son. Isaiah 9:6 certainly does *not* predict that the Messiah would someday *become* the Son of God.

Proverbs 30:4 clearly makes mention of God's Son and this verse is not prophetic. It poses a series of questions concerning the Creator: "Who hath ascended up into heaven, or descended? who hath gathered the wind in his fists? who hath bound the waters in a garment? who hath established all the ends of the earth? what is his name, and what is his son's name, if thou canst tell?"

Little is said of the Trinity in the Old Testament but there are important hints (such as Genesis 1:26; Psalm 110:1; Isaiah 6:8; 48:16; 61:1; 63:9-10). Likewise although the Sonship of Christ finds its full revelation on the pages of the New Testament, the Old Testament is not totally silent about God's Son. The verse cited above (Proverbs 30:4) is an example. A normal and natural reading of this verse leads to the obvious conclusion that God has a Son, not that God would at some future time have a Son. Charles Bridges wrote a masterful and classic commentary on the book of Proverbs and his comments on this verse are worthy of note:

> There is a Son in the Eternal Godhead; a Son, not begotten in time, but from eternity (Prov. 8:22-23); his name therefore, not as some would have it, a component part of his humiliation, but the manifestation of his Godhead: co-existent with his Father in the same ineffable nature, yet personally distinct.[5]

Christ has eternally existed as the Son, but only in the mind of God.

Some people who are opposed to eternal Sonship teach that while Christ did not actually become the Son until the incarnation, He was eternally the Son in the mind of God; that is, God always knew and purposed that the second person of the Trinity would someday become the Son of God. In God's mind it was settled and certain, although it did not come to pass historically until the incarnation.

To support this objection people point to the expression *the Lamb of God.* In the mind and purpose of God even before creation Christ was the Lamb that was slain, although He did not actually and historically become the Lamb of God until His sacrificial and substitutionary death on Calvary's cross. Before the world ever existed it was settled and certain that the second person of the Trinity would die for sinful men. He was "the Lamb slain from the foundation of the world" (Revelation 13:8). In a similar way could we not also speak of the Son of God as pre-existing in the mind and counsels of God and yet not actually becoming the Son until the incarnation?

On the surface this argument seems plausible but we must not miss an important distinction. The expression *Lamb of God* points us to our Lord's historical sacrificial work accomplished on the cross when He died as our sinless substitute. The expression *Son of God* is very different in that it describes our Lord's eternal relationship to His Father. *Lamb of God* points to Christ's work, but *Son of God* describes His person. Christ is the second person of the Trinity, eternally related to His Father as Son. The Lamb who was slain is none other than the eternal Son who became a man so that He might "taste death for every man" (Hebrews 2:9).

Hebrews 1:4-5 teaches that Christ obtained the name "Son" at the incarnation: "Being made so much better than the angels, as he hath by inheritance obtained a more excellent name than they. For unto which of the angels said he at any time, Thou art my Son, this day have I begotten thee? And again, I will be to him a Father, and he shall be to me a Son?"

It is assumed by those who teach this view that "this day have I begotten thee" refers to the incarnation at which time Christ obtained the more excellent name of "Son" (a name that was not His prior to His birth in Bethlehem).[6]

Yet to do justice to the context of this passage, we must understand it as a reference not to Christ's incarnation but to His resurrection and exaltation. Hebrews 1:3-4 states, "When he had by himself purged our sins, [He] sat down on the right hand of the Majesty on high; Being made so much better than the angels . . . "

As God, our Lord has always been superior to the angels. In His deity He did not obtain a more excellent name than the angels because as God He always possessed a more excellent name. Indeed He is their infinitely superior Creator (Colossians 1:16). By becoming a man at the incarnation, Christ assumed a position inferior to that of the angels as Hebrews 2:9 reveals: "But we see Jesus, who was made a little lower than the angels for the suffering of death." At His exaltation He obtained a higher position and a more excellent name than the angels as Paul tells us in Ephesians 1:20-21: "Which he wrought in Christ, when he [God] raised him from the dead, and set him at his own right hand in the heavenly places, Far above all principality, and power, and might, and dominion, and every name that is named, not only in this world, but also in that which is to come." As believers we share with Christ in His exalted position because we are seated in heavenly places with Him (Ephesians 2:6).

It is wrong to say that Hebrews 1:4-5 refers to the incarnation because the context is speaking of Christ's exaltation (1:3). It is also wrong to say that at His exaltation Christ became the Son of God. He was clearly identified as God's Son prior to His exaltation—at His transfiguration

(Matthew 17:5), at His baptism (Matthew 3:17), and at His birth (Luke 1:32,35). Indeed the author of Hebrews declared that by the Son the worlds were made (Hebrews 1:2), thus making it certain that Christ existed as God's Son even at the time of creation.

The term "Son" primarily signifies submission, obedience, subservience, and even inferiority.

In Jewish usage the term *son* did not generally imply subjection and subordination, but rather equality and identity of nature.[7] When the Lord Jesus claimed to be the Son of God, the Jews did not say, "You are making Yourself to be inferior and subservient to God." They clearly understood that the Lord was claiming for Himself equality with God (John 5:17-18). Even on the human plane, *son* does not always convey the idea of subjection:

> The term "Son" only "denotes subjection" in childhood and in the adolescent stage, before maturity is reached. When full-grown or fully developed, the son is competent to represent the father, because he corresponds in nature and qualities with the father. The son, therefore, in normal conditions, is considered not inferior but equal to the father, and able to maintain the prestige of the family.[8]

Hebrews 5:8 contains the ideas of both Sonship and subjection. Notice how they are contrasted: "Though he were a Son, yet learned he obedience by the things which he suffered." This verse teaches that Christ existed as a Son. It does not say, "When He became a Son, He learned obedience." Hocking explained this passage well:

> The truth is that the new theory which claims that "sonship" denotes subjection confuses the scriptural

distinction between "son" and "servant." Subjection is a feature which is essential to the character of a servant, but exceptional and voluntary in the case of a son. A son may consent to become a servant, but a servant cannot elevate himself to become a son. . . . Subjection was foreign to the nature of the Eternal Son, yet He learned obedience when incarnate. The absurdity of the assertion that subjection is denoted by the word "Son" is seen at once when applied to this passage, substituting those words for the word "Son." The statement of the Messianic glory is converted into a mere platitude by this change: "Though He were *in subjection,* yet learned He obedience from the things which He suffered." How commonplace! The one who is subject *must* obey. The emphatic force of "though," which means "notwithstanding the fact that," is lost. The glory of the obedient Son has departed from the passage when the eternity of the Sonship is denied![9]

Another important difference between Son and servant is shown in the contrast between Christ and Moses in Hebrews 3:5-6: "Moses verily was faithful in all his house, as a servant . . . But Christ [was faithful] as a son over his own house."

Praise be to the Son! He who was equal with God willingly emptied and humbled Himself, being obedient to the Father's will even to the point of submitting to a shameful death on the cross (Philippians 2:6-8). Although He was God's eternal Son, He became our servant, our Savior, and our substitute. The majesty of His condescension is not that the eternal God became Son. The majesty lies in the fact that the exalted Son of God laid aside His heavenly glory and became a man so that He by the grace of God might "taste death for every man" (Hebrews 2:9). Let us not seek to exalt His condescension by degrading His Sonship.

The second person of the Trinity took on a new function, assumed a new role, and received a new name and title that He did not previously possess.

To refute this objection to eternal Sonship, we must make a careful and clear distinction between who a person is and a title he may receive, a function he may assume, or a role he may play. For example let us say that Mr. Samuel Jones is the son of Mr. Thomas Jones. Many things about Mr. Samuel Jones could change. He could work for a new employer or be promoted to a new position. He could receive a new title such as vice-president of the bank. None of these changes, however, would alter his basic identity as the son of Mr. Thomas Jones. So how can it be said that Sonship was just a role that Christ played and a function that He assumed? How can it be taught that *Son* was His incarnate title and a new name that He never before possessed?

What does the Scripture say? Does it not call Christ God's "own Son" (Romans 8:3)? Is He not the Father's proper and peculiar Son, His own in a sense different and distinct from any other? Does Scripture not speak of Him as the Father's "beloved," "wellbeloved," and "only begotten" Son? If such expressions do not indicate an actual relationship—that Christ is indeed the true, real, proper, and unique Son of the Father—what could these words possibly mean?[10] As to His very person, He is God's Son, the One who is distinct from the Father yet equal in nature. W. J. Ouweneel noted the following important distinction:

> "Son (of God)" is a *name,* and not a title (such as King). The distinction between these two things is this: a name belongs to a person, but a title belongs to an office. A name gives expression of *who* a person is; a title expresses *what* he is. Thus in Psalm 2 Christ is called King (this tells us what He is) and

He is called Son (which tells us who He is). The first
thing is an "official" matter and the second a personal one.... Sonship is not an office. It is definitely
objectionable to refer to the expression "Son" as a
title.[11]

If being the Son of God involves Christ's real, true, and
proper relationship with the Father as a distinct person in
the godhead who shares the Father's divine nature, then
certainly His Sonship must be as eternal as His relationship
to the Father. To say that Christ became the Son at the
incarnation is to say that prior to this there did not exist a
Father/Son relationship in the godhead. But there could
never be a time when He was not the Son because there
could never be a time when He was other than the person
He is—the Father's beloved and only begotten Son. He is
"the same yesterday, and to day, and for ever" (Hebrews
13:8). To understand the doctrine of eternal Sonship correctly it is essential to recognize that His Sonship directly
relates to His essential nature and identity. *Son of God* is
not merely a role or a title that Christ assumed in time.

**The concept of eternal generation is erroneous and
therefore the doctrine of eternal Sonship is erroneous.**

Opponents of eternal Sonship object to the idea of
eternal generation. Indeed, a common approach is to attack
the doctrine of eternal Sonship by attacking eternal generation.

Some of the objections against eternal generation are
well founded. *Eternal generation,* a theological term that
does not occur in the Bible, refers to a concept that is used
to attempt to describe and explain the doctrine of eternal
Sonship, which is difficult for finite and frail men to
understand. The idea of eternal Sonship is well beyond the
range of our experience because we do not know of any son

who did not have a beginning and birth. But some of the arguments in support of eternal generation are weak and lack Biblical support. For example, many proponents of eternal generation employ a very questionable exegesis of Psalm 2:7 (understanding "this day" as a reference to some kind of mystical "eternal day"). Others totally misunderstand the term *only begotten,* which is found in John 3:16 (the term really means "one of a kind, unique").

Those who reject eternal Sonship must also reject eternal generation. Those who firmly hold to eternal Sonship do not necessarily accept the entire concept of eternal generation.[12]

The denial of eternal Sonship cannot be successfully substantiated with Scripture. The incarnational Sonship position is weighed in the balance and found lacking. The virgin birth of Christ was certainly a key event in the history of redemption, but it did not mark the beginning of the Father/Son relationship in the godhead. Christ's Sonship is from everlasting. "Now unto the King eternal, immortal, invisible, the only wise God, be honour and glory for ever and ever. Amen" (1 Timothy 1:17).

Chapter 10

THE NECESSITY AND IMPORTANCE OF THE DOCTRINE

But these are written, that ye might believe that Jesus is the Christ, the Son of God; and that believing ye might have life through his name. . . . Who is he that overcometh the world, but he that believeth that Jesus is the Son of God? (John 20:31; 1 John 5:5)

Certainly the concept of Sonship is central to our faith. The Father's gift of love to this world is His only begotten Son (John 3:16). God commands us to believe on the name of His Son (1 John 3:23). We must confess, "We believe and are sure that thou art that Christ, the Son of the living God" (John 6:69). If a person is condemned it is because he has not believed in the name of the only begotten Son of God (John 3:18). "He that believeth on the Son hath everlasting life: and he that believeth not the Son shall not see life; but the wrath of God abideth on him" (John 3:36). The person who has the Son has eternal life (1 John 5:11-12). With ceaseless thanksgiving we can praise the Father for delivering us from the power of darkness and translating us into the kingdom of His dear Son (Colossians 1:13). All of the preceding pivotal statements revolve around the Sonship of Christ, and it is

essential that our concept of His Sonship be in full harmony with God's revelation.

What should our attitude be with regard to the denial
of the doctrine of eternal Sonship? How critical is this
issue? How important is this doctrine? How dangerous is
the view which supposes that our Lord became the Son of
God at some point in history? Should we consider those
who hold such a view to be sound in the faith? Should we
tolerate this view as orthodox?

There are those today who do not consider the doctrine of eternal Sonship to be an important issue. They say
that if a person strongly believes in the deity of Christ, the
pre-existence of Christ, and the triune godhead, whether or
not he believes in eternal Sonship is a minor matter (a mere
technicality or matter of terminology). They say that those
who deny and those who affirm eternal Sonship are both
within the orthodox camp and should be considered sound
in the faith. They argue, "Why does it really matter since we
all agree that Jesus Christ is the Son of God both now and
forevermore?"

Others have embraced the doctrine of eternal Sonship
and believe it to be a vital Bible doctrine that must not be
compromised. During the past century many in the Plymouth Brethren assemblies have valiantly defended this
doctrine and have broken fellowship over this issue as they
deemed necessary.[1] Many doctrinal statements of churches,
Bible schools, and mission agencies declare that Jesus
Christ is the eternal Son of God, and the inclusion of this
point in such documents indicates that this doctrine is
considered important and an integral part of "those things
which are most surely believed among us" (Luke 1:1).

Of historical interest is the case of Calvin and the
intolerant Swiss reformers in the days when Servetus was
burned at the stake for his heretical teaching regarding the
Trinity. The controversy centered on his denial of the
doctrine of eternal Sonship:

> When Servetus heard of the unexpected sentence of
> death, he was horror-struck. . . . The venerable old
> Farel visited him in the prison at seven in the
> morning, and remained with him till the hour of his
> death. He tried to convince him of his error. Servetus
> asked him to quote a single Scripture passage where
> Christ was called "Son of God" *before* his incarna-
> tion. Farel could not satisfy him.[2]

Servetus was taken to the stake to be burned. The
account continues:

> The flames soon reach him and consume his mortal
> frame in the forty-fourth year of his fitful life. In the
> last moment he is heard to pray, in smoke and
> agony, with a loud voice: "Jesus Christ, thou Son of
> the eternal God, have mercy upon me!" This was at
> once a confession of his faith and of his error. He
> could not be induced, says Farel, to confess that
> Christ was the *eternal* Son of God.[3]

It is one thing to condemn error but quite another thing
to put the offender to death. Obviously we do not recom-
mend the execution of those who deny the doctrine of
eternal Sonship.[4] Some of these men we hold in high es-
teem. We appreciate their Bible-centered teaching in other
areas and the contributions they have made by way of
pulpit and pen. At the same time we dare not minimize the
importance of sound doctrine as it relates to the person of
God's Son. We must give our hearty "Amen" to what the Spirit
of God teaches us in the Word of God about the Son of God.

God's people living in this present church age have a
definite responsibility with respect to false doctrine and
erroneous teaching. God's truth must ever be jealously
guarded. Our hearts need to be right and our teaching needs
to be sound: "Take heed unto thyself, and unto the doctrine"

(1 Timothy 4:16; also see Acts 20:28). Our God-given responsibility to preserve doctrinal purity demands we take the following seven steps:

1. Test all things by the Word of God. "Prove all things; hold fast that which is good" (1 Thessalonians 5:21). The inerrant Word of God is the objective standard by which we are to test all things. In our day there are many winds of doctrine (Ephesians 4:14) and these must be examined and scrutinized according to God's perfect standard of truth. God's people need to be very discerning as they read books, listen to taped messages, hear radio broadcasts, and view religious television programs. We must ask ourselves how each teaching lines up with God's Word. Is the teaching truth that we can hold fast or is it error that must be rejected? May the blessed Spirit of God give us keen minds to discern between truth and error so that we do not embrace any opinion or viewpoint that is contrary to the mind of the Lord, even if such an opinion is voiced by a highly-respected Bible teacher.

2. Indoctrinate God's people. Such was the ministry of the apostle Paul: "I have not shunned to declare unto you all the counsel of God" (Acts 20:27). God's people need to be immersed in a program of total indoctrination. The devil himself knows the importance of indoctrination. The average Jehovah's Witness, for example, is ready always to give an answer to every man that asks him a reason of the false hope that is within him. The average Bible-believer is horribly ignorant of God's truth. Many believers would have difficulty proving from the Scriptures even the basic truth that Jesus Christ is God. Many local churches function as evangelistic centers instead of edification centers. People are taught how to be saved, and for this we thank God, but believers are not being built up in the most holy faith. They are thus doctrinally illiterate and totally unprepared to evaluate properly a deviant doctrinal viewpoint such as the Sonship-by-incarnation theory. The more we understand the truth about the person of Christ, the more we will be able to detect that which is false. One Bible teacher said that "the best defense against false teaching is a thoroughly biblical Christology."[5]

3. Expose erroneous teaching. Paul did this repeatedly in his Epistles. He exposed the false teaching of Hymenaeus and Philetus, who erred with respect to the resurrection (2 Timothy 2:17-18). When necessary Paul would name names. Today we are sometimes told that our ministry should be positive and loving and we should not cause division in the body of Christ by pointing out doctrinal differences. Dr. John MacArthur, in dealing with the modern charismatic movement, spoke well to this issue:

> That kind of thinking sacrifices truth for the sake of a superficial peace. Such an attitude pervades the contemporary church. . . . It is *not* unkind to analyze doctrinal differences in the light of Scripture. It is not necessarily factious to voice disagreement with someone else's teaching. In fact, we have a moral imperative to examine what is proclaimed in Jesus' name, and to expose and condemn false teaching and unbiblical behavior. The apostle Paul felt it necessary at times to rebuke people by name in epistles meant to be read publicly (Phil. 4:2-3; 1 Tim. 1:20; 2 Tim. 2:17).[6]

We should expose those who hold an erroneous view regarding the person of God the Holy Spirit. We must do the same with those who hold an erroneous view regarding the person of the Son.

4. Warn God's people. We dare not depreciate the importance of a warning ministry. God forbid that those who stand in the pulpits today should be timid sentinels. Again Paul is our example: "Therefore watch, and remember, that by the space of three years I ceased not to warn every one night and day with tears" (Acts 20:31). Merely to teach God's people "positive" truth without giving warning is to fatten the sheep for the wolves who will not spare the flock (Acts 20:29-30).

Are believers immune to dangers? Are they safe from contamination by subtle errors? Is doctrinal defection an impossibility? Has the god of this age lost all control and influence over our minds? If these questions can be answered in the affirmative, then a ministry of warning is totally unnecessary.

5. Demand doctrinal integrity. If a church, mission agency, school, or organization has a doctrinal statement that is based on the clear teachings of the Bible, this document must be upheld by those in leadership. Honesty and integrity require that they believe just what they say they believe. Those who sign the doctrinal statement must do so only if they are in hearty agreement with the entire document. Membership must be denied to any who are not in hearty agreement with the statement of faith. Consistency and doctrinal integrity demand this. If the doctrinal statement does not accurately reflect the teaching of the Bible, the statement should be changed so that it is an accurate representation of "those things which are most surely believed among us" (Luke 1:1).

Not too many years ago the director of a mission made it known that he no longer embraced the pretribulation-rapture position.[7] This change in his thinking put him in conflict with the doctrinal statement of the mission he directed. He could no longer be in wholehearted agreement with the statement of faith. The board of the mission had to make a decision. They could follow the wishes of the director and change the doctrinal statement to allow for his new view on the rapture, or they could abide by their stated doctrinal position. They refused to change and as a result the director felt he had to resign. The director was wrong to abandon the Biblical doctrine of the pretribulation rapture, but he was right to remove himself from the mission since he could no longer sign the doctrinal statement.

If a doctrinal statement says, "We believe that the Lord Jesus Christ is the eternal Son of God," how can a person sign the statement if he denies the eternal Sonship of Christ? To be consistent, a person should not sign such a doctrinal statement if he holds the Sonship-by-incarnation view. Inconsistency is serious and the issue becomes even more serious when a person's published writings set forth a doctrine that contradicts the clear doctrinal statement of the organization of which he is a part.[8]

The doctrinal integrity of an organization is compromised when its leaders knowingly allow and tolerate deviant and contrary doctrines that contradict the clear wording of the official doctrinal position. In effect such leaders are saying that the doctrinal statement does not really mean what it says. This approach is dangerous. It makes the doctrinal statement a meaningless document. Norman L. Geisler made the following keen observation:

> This is precisely how denominations go liberal, namely, when their doctrinal statements are stretched beyond their original meaning to accommodate new doctrinal deviations. . . . We cannot allow this crucial doctrine [of the bodily resurrection] to be watered down by accommodating deviant views, no matter how much we personally like those who hold these positions. The simple truth is that brotherly charity should not be used as an excuse to neglect doctrinal purity. Eternal vigilance is the price for orthodoxy. . . . It is a sad day indeed

when we allow the original meaning of our doctrines to be changed without ever permitting the
church representatives to vote on it.[9]

The well-documented case of Fuller Seminary's departure from the doctrine of Biblical inerrancy illustrates
what happens when doctrinal integrity is compromised.[10]
Fuller's original doctrinal statement was very clear. The
Bible was said to be "free from all error in the whole and in
the part." One professor could not honestly sign that part
of the statement of faith and as a result he left the institu-
tion. There were, however, other professors who signed the
statement of faith even though they did not believe in the
doctrine of inerrancy. They clearly violated doctrinal integrity. How can a doctrinal statement have any credibility
if those signing it have mental reservations and do not
really believe what they sign? The statement becomes a
meaningless document. About a decade after the controversy began, Fuller Seminary changed its doctrinal statement so that it no longer said "free from all error." The
leaven of doctrinal compromise leavened the whole lump.
Spiritual leaders must not tolerate and must not ac-
commodate doctrinal positions that are contrary to God's
Word and contrary to their organization's stated doctrinal
position. Integrity and honesty demand that we hold fast to
what we have said we believe. Even God's Word is of no
profit if we refuse to believe it, adhere to it, and practice it
(Hebrews 4:2). Paul's exhortation to Timothy is appropri-
ate: "Hold fast the form of sound words, which thou hast
heard of me, in faith and love which is in Christ Jesus" (2
Timothy 1:13).

6. *Speak the truth in love.* The apostle Paul spoke of the
importance of believers being unified in the knowledge of
the Son of God: "Till we all come in the unity of the faith,
and of the knowledge of the Son of God, unto a perfect man,

unto the measure of the stature of the fulness of Christ" (Ephesians 4:13). The unity that believers possess and enjoy is based on truth and this truth centers in the person of the Son of God. In this context Paul stated the necessity of "speaking the truth in love" so that believers might "grow up into him in all things, which is the head, even Christ" (Ephesians 4:15).

There are many today who minimize the importance of Bible doctrine by saying that the only thing that really matters is love. They say that what we believe does not matter as long as we love each other. To them the mark of true orthodoxy is love, not doctrine. They say that if we truly love each other, we will not allow ourselves to be divided over doctrinal matters. They think that if believers are to win the world for Christ, they must bury their differences and proclaim the essential core of the gospel in a positive way.

Should we really sacrifice truth and sound doctrine for the sake of love, tolerance, peace, and unity? Does not true love rejoice in the truth (1 Corinthians 13:6)? The apostle John often spoke of love in his Epistles, but he also issued very strong words against those who did not abide in the correct doctrine of Christ (2 John 7-11). Preaching the gospel is essential, but if we are careless about truth and doctrine, even the gospel we proclaim is in jeopardy. The gospel message centers in the person of Jesus Christ the Son of God (Romans 1:1-4). How can we preach Christ in a God-honoring way if we do not jealously guard the truth concerning Christ and who He is? The gospel message must ever be "according to the scriptures" (1 Corinthians 15:3-4).

Bible doctrine is extremely important. Souls are saved and believers are sanctified and unified on the basis of God's truth (James 1:18; John 17:17; Ephesians 4:13-15). If we truly love a person, we will desire that person to be totally indoctrinated in the truth of God from Genesis to Revelation. True unity is enjoyed only as believers enter into a common understanding of the Word of God. From God's perspective those who are hindering the cause of Christian unity are those who refuse to stand faithfully and obediently upon the written Word of God. God's truth must prevail. "But speak thou the things which become sound doctrine" (Titus 2:1).

7. Protect the doctrinal purity of the local assembly of believers. (The same imperative would of course apply to schools and mission agencies.) Error must be dealt with. It must not be ignored. It must not be tolerated or minimized. Those who are teaching error must be confronted in an honest, loving, and Biblical manner. Godly church leaders need to protect the local church from devious error: "Take heed therefore unto yourselves, and to all the flock, over the which the Holy Ghost hath made you overseers, to feed the church of God, which he hath purchased with his own blood. For I know this, that after my departing shall grievous wolves enter in among you, not sparing the flock. Also of your own selves shall men arise, speaking perverse things, to draw away disciples after them" (Acts 20:28-30).

Doctrinal error enters churches in very subtle and seemingly innocuous ways. Dr. Ironside recognized this fact and issued this admonition:

> It is always right to stand firmly for what God has revealed concerning His blessed Son's person and work. The father of lies deals in half-truths, and specializes in most subtle fallacies concerning the Lord Jesus, our sole and sufficient Saviour.[11]

Departure from God's Word may be at first very slight and difficult to discern. For this reason many have failed to see the problems and dangers of the incarnational Sonship position. Many who deny eternal Sonship still believe in the deity of Christ. They believe in the pre-existence or eternality of Christ. They believe in the three persons of the Trinity who have eternally existed. Is their concept of Christ's Sonship really a serious problem? Is it insidious error that if left unchecked will damage the body of Christ?

To deny our Lord's true, essential, proper, unique, eternal, and inherent relationship with the Father *is* serious error. We must not approve of the teaching that says the Father/Son relationship was nonexistent prior to the incarnation. We must not rob the second person of the Trinity of His essential identity as the beloved and eternal Son of the Father (Colossians 1:13). We must strongly oppose any teaching that says that His Sonship has nothing to do with His essential nature and essence. This is the very heart of the eternal Sonship issue.

Denial of eternal Sonship may appear to be only a slight deviation but the error can lead to more serious departure from the truth. False teaching is dangerous not only because it misrepresents facts on which one's faith is to be fixed; false teaching can also lead one in the wrong direction and influence others to stray. One person who accepts a false view of Christ could open the door for another person to hold an even more dangerous view. Christians have a responsibility to guard the truth concerning Christ's Sonship in order to help others avoid even more serious error.

If left unchecked, the denial of the doctrine of eternal Sonship *will* damage the body of Christ. We can work to prevent such damage by defending the doctrine, and we can defend the doctrine by pointing out the problems facing those who deny it. There are at least ten problems:

1. Those who deny eternal Sonship are proposing a view that is contrary to the plain teaching of the Bible.[12] They deny what the Scriptures assert: that Christ is the eternal Son. They also assert what the Scriptures deny: that He became the Son at the incarnation or at some other point in history. Unbiblical teaching of any kind must be taken seriously, and much more so when dealing with a subject as important as the person of Christ and His relationship with the Father.

It is crucial that we give a clear and correct answer to our Lord's question, "But whom say ye that I am?" (Matthew 16:15). Every believer must acknowledge (confess) the Son (1 John 2:23). We must acknowledge that Jesus Christ is exactly who God says He is. God the Father has testified concerning His Son (1 John 5:9), and we need to be in full agreement with this testimony. In His Word the Father has given clear and ample testimony regarding His eternal Son, and it is neither wise nor safe to deny or disagree with what God has said.

2. Those who deny eternal Sonship must change the normal and natural meaning of many key passages of Scripture, often robbing the text of its force or true significance. The following are a few examples of how certain verses would need to be paraphrased to fit the Sonship-by-incarnation view:

Colossians 1:13,16—All things were created by the Son, who was not truly the Son until thousands of years after the time of creation.

John 3:16—God so loved the world that He gave the One who became His only begotten Son at the time of the incarnation.

John 3:17—God sent His Son into the world to be the Savior, although the One who was sent did not actually become the Son until the incarnation.

John 16:28—The Lord Jesus came forth from the

Father, who was not actually His Father until He had come forth.

John 17:24—The Father loved the Son before the foundation of the world, although at that time a Father/Son relationship did not yet exist.

1 John 1:1-2—In the beginning the One who is eternal life was with the Father, although in the beginning He was not yet the Son and the Father was not yet the Father.

John 1:18—Before the foundation of the world the One we now know as the Son was in the bosom of the One we now know as the Father, delighting in the love of the One who would someday become His Father at the incarnation.

3. Those who deny eternal Sonship teach that Christ's Sonship has no bearing whatever on the issue of Christ's essential nature. They thus divorce Christ's Sonship from the person He is. When speaking of the Son they emphasize *who He became* rather than *who He is.* They say that He *became* the Son, insisting that before the incarnation He was not the Son.

Before the incarnation Jesus Christ existed as the second person of the Trinity in all of the inherent fullness and glory of His blessed person. He was everything the eternal God should be. If He were not the Son prior to His coming into this world, we would conclude that Sonship bears no real intrinsic relationship to His eternal person because He could be exactly who He is and yet not be the Son. According to this view Sonship must be external, extrinsic, and extraneous to the real, true, proper, and essential essence of who Jesus Christ really is.

In contrast to the incarnational Sonship view, the

Bible teaches that the Sonship of Jesus Christ involves the very person and nature of our Lord, the essence of who He is as the second person of the Trinity. Since He can never become other than who He is, He can never exist apart from being the Son. We must not divorce His Sonship from His person. He is the same yesterday, today, and forever (Hebrews 13:8) and He is the Son yesterday, today, and forever. To say that He once existed without being the Son of God is to say that He once was other than who He really is. The Gospel of John was written so that we might believe that Jesus is the Son of God (John 20:31). It was not written so that we might believe that He became the Son of God when He assumed the role of Son. He *is* the Son.

4. *Those who deny eternal Sonship insult the person of Christ by making His Sonship merely a role, title, office, function, or name that He assumed.* They refuse to recognize Sonship as part of His real, actual, and intrinsic nature. They rob Him of His true identity. They insist that *Son of God* was merely a title He acquired, a role He played, a name He took on, and a function that He assumed at the time of the incarnation. They deny that He is really, truly, actually, properly, intrinsically, and eternally the beloved Son of the Father. According to their view Christ is the Son not because of who He is essentially and ontologically, but because of what He became and what He did. Their teaching with respect to the Father is the same. They say that the first person of the Trinity received the title and took on the role of Father at the incarnation.

Yet the Bible never refers to Christ's Sonship as a title or as a role. Scripture calls it a *name:* "Because he hath not believed in the name of the only begotten Son of God" (John 3:18). *Son* is an essential name, a name that has ever been His, a name that relates to His essential nature and essence. When Peter said, "Thou art the Christ, the Son of the living God" (Matthew 16:16), he was not acknowledging a mere title or role. He was declaring who Jesus Christ really and truly and essentially is.

The eternal Sonship position insists that His Sonship is His essential identity, the very essence of who He is. The incarnational Sonship view detracts from the fullness of the essence of the Lord Jesus Christ. Do we dare offend the second person of the triune God by saying that His Sonship bears no relationship to His essential identity and essence?

5. Those who deny eternal Sonship misunderstand the basic significance of the expression "Son of God." They teach that the primary significance of Sonship is that of submission, subservience, obedience, and even inferiority. They confuse Sonship with servitude, whereas the Bible contrasts these two concepts (Hebrews 5:8; 3:5-6). They understand the expression *Son of God* to be an incarnate title, referring to a name He assumed and a role He played when He became a man.

The New Testament makes it abundantly evident that *Son of God* denotes equality, not inferiority (John 5:17-18). To claim to be the Son of God was to claim to be of the same nature as God—to be one with God. Whereas the term *Son of man* refers to Jesus' humanity, the term *Son of God* emphasizes His full deity. The Lord Jesus did not become the Son of God at His incarnation; He became the Son of man. To understand the term *Son of God* as an incarnate title or role meaning "subservient to God" is a grave mistake.[13]

6. Those who deny eternal Sonship also deny eternal fatherhood. If Christ was not always the Son, then the first person of the Trinity was not always the Father. He cannot exist as Father apart from the Son. As Dr. John Walvoord correctly stated, "If Christ became a Son by means of the incarnation and was not a Son before that event, then the Father was not a Father of the Lord Jesus before the incarnation."[14] Those who deny eternal Sonship, then, believe that the Son was not the Son and the Father was not the Father until the incarnation. This is strange doctrine when we consider that the third person of the Trinity was clearly identified as the Spirit of God thousands of years before the incarnation (Genesis 1:2).

7. *Those who deny eternal Sonship imply that in the eternal ages prior to the incarnation there was a nameless Trinity.* If we follow their logic, there are no Bible names by which we can identify the persons of the Trinity in eternity past. How then do we identify and speak of God prior to the creation of the universe? What names do we use to identify the persons of the Trinity? If the second person was not the Son, who was He? The same could be asked concerning the Father.

According to this false view, not only would we have to say the Trinity was nameless; we would also be forced to say that God has not chosen to reveal Himself as He really is, but only as He was pleased to become.[15] The triune God, according to this view, has revealed only the titles and roles He would assume; He has not revealed Himself as He really is.

8. *Those who deny eternal Sonship fail to explain the nature of the relationship that existed in past ages between the first and second persons of the godhead.* Dr. Walvoord said the view that begins Christ's Sonship at the incarnation leaves "unexplained the mystery of the relation of the first Person to the second Person—indeed why the titles and order are justified."[16] Prior to the creation of the universe, what relationship existed between the persons of the Trinity? Those who reject the idea of eternal Sonship often refer to the *first person* and the *second person*. These terms however are not found in the Bible. Furthermore these theological terms are derived from the doctrine of eternal Sonship and lose their meaning apart from this doctrine. Because an eternal relationship existed between the Father and Son, we can refer to the first person (Father) and second person (Son). Being able to rank the persons first, second, and third is possible only because God has revealed Himself as the one triune God, eternally existing in three persons—Father, Son, and Holy Spirit.[17]

9. Those who deny eternal Sonship are paving the way for the teaching that the persons of the Trinity could have been interchangeable. This teaching says that the Father could have been the Son, the Spirit could have been the Father, the Son could have been the Spirit, etc. If *Son* and *Father* are merely roles and titles, there is no reason why these roles and titles could not have been interchanged. Philpot explained it this way:

> If Father, Son and Holy Ghost are mere names and titles, distinct from and independent of their very mode of subsistence, the Holy Ghost might have been the Father and sent the Son, or the Son might have been the Father . . . for if the three Persons of the Trinity are three distinct subsistences, independent of each other, and have no such mutual and eternal relationship as these very names imply, there seems to be no reason why these titles might not have been interchanged . . . for certainly if they are three equal, independent Persons, at liberty to choose Their several titles, there appears to be no reason why They should not have chosen otherwise than They did . . . the Father might have been the Son, and the Son might have been the Father, etc. . . . We see therefore, into what confusion men get when they forsake the simple statements of Scripture.[18]

God is not the author of confusion (1 Corinthians 14:33)!

10. Those who deny eternal Sonship are paving the way for the teaching that says that Jesus Christ was once less than God. Thankfully many who teach that Christ became the Son by means of incarnation recoil in horror from the thought that He was ever less than God, and yet this is what their teaching implies.

The New Testament makes it very clear that the expression *Son of God* was a declaration of deity. At the trial of Christ the key issue was whether or not He was the Son of God. When Jesus affirmed His divine Sonship, He was condemned to die for blasphemy (Matthew 26:63-65; Luke 22:70; John 19:7). He was claiming to be equal with God (John 5:18)! He was claiming to share God's divine nature. To say, "I am the Son of God," was the same as saying, "I am God. I am of the same nature as the Father. I and my Father are one."

Despite these claims to deity, those who deny eternal Sonship insist that Christ *became* God's Son at some point in history. The implications of this view need to be carefully weighed. Suppose a man correctly understands *Son of God* as an expression that points to the full deity of Christ. The man knows that Christ as God's Son is a distinct person from the Father yet shares the same divine nature as the Father. If the man is then told that Jesus Christ *became* God's Son and that there was a time when He was not the Son of God, what will his conclusion be? The man will think that since *Son of God* means equality with God, there must have been a time when Christ was not equal with God, when He was less than God, not fully possessing the divine nature. The implication is that He became full deity and of the same nature as God at the time of His incarnation; prior to His becoming the Son, He must have been less than full deity. Thus denial of Christ's eternal Sonship can lead to denial of the full and eternal deity of Christ.

Because of these ten problems it is essential that God's

people hold firmly to the doctrine of eternal Sonship without wavering. This truth involves the person and essential identity of our blessed Savior and must never be surrendered. The doctrine is important and it is vital. It is essential truth relating to who Jesus Christ really is. In discussing the differences between incarnational Sonship and eternal Sonship we are not dealing with mere technicalities or semantics. We are dealing with two opposing positions. The one presents His Sonship as merely a role or a title that He assumed at the incarnation. The other position points to His true person and identifies Him by His eternal relationship in the godhead. May the living God open the eyes of our understanding "till we all come in the unity of the faith, and of the knowledge of the Son of God, unto a perfect man, unto the measure of the stature of the fulness of Christ" (Ephesians 4:13).

The Lord Jesus Christ is God's unique and beloved Son from all eternity. Long before the universe ever was, the Son of God was basking in the sunlight of His Father's love, resting in the joy of His Father's bosom, and delighting in the blessedness of His Father's fellowship. The Son was distinct in personality from the Father yet was one in nature, sharing all the attributes of deity. In the fullness of time the Father sent forth His Son into this world on a saving mission (Galatians 4:4; John 3:17). "Herein is love, not that we loved God, but that he loved us, and sent his Son to be the propitiation for our sins" (1 John 4:10). Blessed be His name! May all those who love the Savior join in ascribing honor and glory to the eternal Son, who is worthy of such both now, in the ages past, and forever.

APPENDIX A

The following article originally appeared in the *Grace Journal*, Spring 1965, Volume 6, Number 2 (pages 16-23) and is used with permission granted by Grace Theological Seminary and by the author.

THE TERM "SON OF GOD" IN THE LIGHT OF OLD TESTAMENT IDIOM

by S. Herbert Bess

The Second Person of the Trinity is frequently referred to in the New Testament as the Son of God (Luke 1:35; John 1:34; 3:18; Acts 9:20; Romans 1:4; et passim). In developing a statement of the doctrine of the Trinity, the early church encountered a problem arising from the use of the word "son." Early church fathers stressed the word *logos,* but when attention shifted more to the term "son," the problem became more acute. The difficulty stems from a too-literal interpretation of the word "son," and from assuming that the expression refers to origin or to generation, rather than to relationship; from understanding the word too much on the analogy of human experience and therefore supposing the existence of a Father who existed prior to the Son.

Church leaders of the third and fourth centuries composed a doctrine of the Trinity and a statement on the nature of Christ which took account of the problem and sought to deal with the word "son" in such a way as to do justice to the deity of Christ as well as to his human nature. This was not done without many conferences and councils, nor without many restatements of doctrine so as to correct heretical views or distortions occasioned by too great a stress on one factor to the neglect of some other. A satisfactory formulation was arrived at finally at the Council of Nicea in 325 A. D., after a long history of discussion and controversy.

The Alexandrian scholar, Origen, had in the preceding century contributed to the formulation of the doctrine when he discussed what he termed the *eternal generation* of the Son. He did not mean by the term, however, exactly what the Nicene theologians later meant by it. For while Origen used the term *eternal generation,* he nonetheless taught that Christ was less than God the Father in respect to *essence.* He maintained that the Son did not participate in the self-subsistent substance of the deity, and he should not be thought of as consubstantial *(homoousios)* with the Father.[1] Origen's inadequate and unfortunate definition of the Sonship of Christ laid the groundwork for the heretical views of Arius and his followers on the nature of Christ. Their heresy is being perpetuated today by the so-called Jehovah's Witnesses.

The Nicene Council in clarifying the doctrine of eternal generation adopted the statement that "the Son is begotten out of the essence of the Father, God of God, Light of Light, very God of very God, begotten not created, consubstantial with the Father *(homoousion tōi patri).*"[2] Exposition of this position and controversy over it proceeded for years following, but the statement stood as the orthodox view on the nature of Christ.

It is not my intention to try to improve on the statement. Rather, I intend to show that the idiomatic usage of the word "son" in the Old Testament supports the above statement and sheds light on it. I believe that such a study will show how Jesus is properly called the Son of God, the term not implying anything about his origin, or that he had an origin. For we must admit that such an expression as "the eternal generation of the Son" is a highly sophisticated concept quite difficult for some professed theologians, to say nothing of the laity. I suggest that an inductive study of the idiomatic use of "son" will make it easier to explain how Jesus is the Son of God, while avoiding the heretical idea that he ever had a beginning.

The word "son" is used in the Old Testament so frequently as to discourage the effort to count the occurrences. In the overwhelming majority of cases it is used in the literal sense of offspring or descendant. In a significant number of cases, however, the word "son" is used in the non-literal sense, indicating a person's profession, his status or circumstance, or his character. Following are some examples of this usage, the number of them being more than sufficient to demonstrate the point, but employed to show how common was this usage among the Israelites.

I. Showing membership in a profession or a guild

1. Sons of the prophets *(b^{e}nē-hann^{e}bî'îm,* 1 Kings 20:35; 2 Kings 2:3 ff.) refer to men belonging to a prophetic band. Likewise, Amos' assertion (Amos 7:14) that he had not been a prophet or the son of a prophet meant that he had not been a member of such a professional group, but God called him to the prophetic office while he was pursuing another line of work.

2. Sons of oil *(b^{e}nē hayyiṣhār,* Zech. 4:14) are ones anointed with oil, in this case members holding the priestly office.

3. Son of the perfumers *(ben-haraqqaḥîm,* Neh. 3:8), a member of the perfumers' trade.

4. Son of the goldsmiths *(ben-haṣṣōrepî,* Neh. 3:31), a goldsmith.

    5. Sons of the gate-keepers (Ezra 2:42) are simply gate-keepers.

    6. Sons of the troop (2 Chron. 25:13) are men of the army.

Non-biblical texts from ancient times make use of the word in the same idiomatic way. The Code of Hammurabi, para. 188, uses the expression "son of an artisan" to refer to a member of the artisan class.[3]

II. Showing participation in a state or condition

    1. Sons of the exile *(bᵉnē haggôlah,* Ezra 4:1; 6:19; etc.) were Jews who had lived in exile but were now returned to the homeland. The expression is equivalent to exiles.

    2. Son of a foreign country *(ben-nēkār,* Gen. 17:12,27; Exod. 12:43) is a foreigner. The term is translated "stranger" in the KJV.

    3. Sons of pledges (2 Kings 14:14) are hostages, and the term is so translated in KJV.

    4. Sons of affliction (Prov. 31:5) are afflicted ones.

    5. Sons of passing away *(bᵉne hᵃlop,* Prov. 31:8), are orphans. The KJV failed to catch the sense of this construction.

    6. Son, or sons, of death (1 Sam. 20:31, Psa. 79:11) refer to those who are condemned to die.

Again, the Code of Hammurabi gives us an example of the non-biblical usage of this idiom. Paragraph 196 refers to the son of a free man and the son of a slave. The expressions may be translated properly as a member of the aristocracy and a member of the slave class.[4]

III. Showing a certain character

    1. Son of valor *(ben-ḥayil,* 1 Sam. 14:52) is simply a brave man. KJV translates the expression "valiant man."

    2. Son of wise ones (Isa. 19:11) refers to one of the wise men.

3. Sons of rebellion (Num. 17:25; 17:10 in English Bible) is properly translated in KJV as "rebels."

4. Son, or sons, of wickedness (Psa. 89:23; 2 Sam. 3:34; 7:10) are wicked people.

5. Son of murder (2 Kings 6:32) denotes a murderer.

6. Sons of foolishness (Job 30:8) refer to senseless people.

7. Sons of no name (Job 30:8), translated in KJV as "children of base men," means a disreputable brood.

8. Son of smiting (Deut. 25:2) signifies a person who deserves to be beaten.

9. Son, or sons, of worthlessness (1 Sam. 25:17; Deut. 13:14, English Bible, v. 13) may be translated "worthless fellow," or "base fellow." The KJV has virtually left the term untranslated when rendering it "son of Belial."

10. Sons of tumult (Jer. 48:45) are tumultuous people.

IV. Possessing a certain nature

The expression "son of man" clearly exhibits the use of the word "son" to show the possession of a certain nature. Numbers 23:19 reads: "God is not a man, that he should lie; neither the son of man, that he should repent. . . ." This part of the verse might be paraphrased as follows: "God is not like a man, who frequently lies; nor does he possess the nature of man, who by reason of his own limitations must often change his mind." In Psa. 8:4 (Hebrew, 5) man and son of man are put in parallel to each other and obviously are used as synonyms. The same is true of Psa. 80:17 (18), and in Job 25:6 and 35:8. In Job 16:21 the phrase "son of man" is translated simply as "man" in the KJV. The term "son of man" is used frequently in Ezekiel as addressed to the prophet (Ezek. 2:1,3; 3:1,3,4,10; 4:16; etc.) and means something like "O man," or "mortal man." The term puts the emphasis on the nature of man.

All the examples in the above categories show that we are being consistent with a well established usage of an Old Testament idiom when we maintain that the expression "Son of God," when applied to Jesus Christ, means possessing the nature of, displaying the qualities of, God. By comparison with Old Testament usage, the term need not refer to his origin.

Some may object that the New Testament was not written in the language of the Old Testament, and that therefore the above examples do not really apply. The obvious answer is that Old Testament thought patterns and Old Testament idioms abound in the New Testament, in spite of the difference in language. This is certainly true of the idiom in question. Below is a table of some of the New Testament examples of the non-literal use of the word "son."

Barnabas (Acts 4:36) was so named because the word literally means "son of consolation." He was called that because he was a consoling person.

Sons of thunder was the appellative applied by Jesus to James and John (Mark 3:17) because it signified something outstanding about their character.

Son of peace (Luke 10:6) refers to a peaceful person.

Sons of Abraham (Gal. 3:7) are those like him in the exercise of faith.

Sons of disobedience (Eph. 2:2) are those characterized by disobedience.

Son of perdition (John 17:12; 2 Thess. 2:3) is the lost one.

It is clear from the above that the New Testament uses the idiom in the same way as the Old Testament, especially when indicating nature or character. We are not misguided then, in applying this connotation to "son" in the term "Son of God."

Since we are dealing then with a Semitic idiom, we can test ourselves for accuracy in the understanding of it as applied to Christ, by observing how the Jews responded or reacted when Jesus taught concerning his relation as Son to the Father. They understood that when Jesus said God was his Father he was making himself equal with God and sought to kill him for it (John 5:18). At another time when Jesus spoke concerning the Father and Son relationship they accused him of blasphemy and would have stoned him, because with such terminology Jesus made himself God (John 10:28-36). Now the enemies of Jesus did not respond this way because they misunderstood his terminology, but because they understood him perfectly well. They knew that when Jesus said he was the Son of God he was claiming to be of the nature of God and equal with God. It was on this basis that they demanded his death in the trial before his crucifixion (John 19:7; Luke 22:70; Mark 14:61-64). We are to understand the expression "Son of God" when applied to Jesus just as his enemies did.

If the term "Son of God" when applied to Jesus is to be taken in the sense not strictly literal, that is to say, if the term when applied to him does not allow for any thought of his having been brought into existence, of his beginning, then certain terms will have to be dealt with which might imply the contrary. I refer to "firstborn," "only begotten," and "begotten."

The Term "Firstborn"

The word "firstborn" is employed in reference to Christ in five places in the New Testament (Rom. 8:29; Col. 1:15,18; Rev. 1:5; Heb. 1:6). Most theologians rightly understand that the word refers to *rank* rather than origin. He is first rank in the whole creation, first rank in the inhabited world, first rank among the resurrected, and first rank among the glorified. None is comparable to him.

This meaning can be illustrated from the Old Testament. In the economy of ancient Israel the eldest son was given preferential treatment. He assumed more responsibility than the others, and was rewarded with honor and given two shares in the family inheritance instead of the single share that each of his younger brothers received. Occasionally, however, the eldest son fell out of favor with his father and was replaced in the favored position by a younger brother. Some examples of this are:

> Joseph, who replaced Reuben (Gen. 4:3, cf. 1 Chron. 5:1,2)
>
> Ephraim, who replaced Manasseh (Gen. 48:13-20)
>
> Jacob, who replaced Esau (Gen. 27)
>
> Solomon, who replaced Adonijah (1 Kings 1:5-53)

Examples can also be adduced from the cuneiform documents from Mesopotamia, particularly from Nuzi.[5]

In such cases as the above the younger became the firstborn, i.e., he attained to first rank. The term will not confuse us if we remember that in the Old Testament it was not always the one born first who became the firstborn. The word is used in this sense of the nation of Israel. Although among the nations of the ancient Near East Israel arrived upon the scene much later than others, God elevated the new nation to the place of the most favored. Therefore He said: "Israel is my son, even my firstborn" (Exod. 4:22). Therefore, in the light of Old Testament usage, when the term "firstborn" is applied to Christ it means that he rightly deserves the preferential share in honor and inheritance; it does not refer to his origin.

The Term "Only Begotten"

The word translated "only begotten" *(monogenēs)* is used nine times in the New Testament. It is used in reference to a certain widow's son (Luke 7:2), to Jairus' only daughter (Luke 8:42), and to another only child (Luke 9:38). It is used five times in reference to Christ (John 1:14,18; 3:16,18; 1 John 4:9), and once in referring back to an Old Testament character (Heb. 11:17).

The Greek translations of the Old Testament (Septuagint, Aquila, Symmachus) also employ the word nine times, each time translating a form of the Hebrew word *yāḥîd.* Each one of these occurrences refers to an only child, seven of them to an only child in the ordinary sense. But twice the term is used of Isaac the son of Abraham (Gen. 22:2, Aquila; 22:12, Symmachus), and these occurrences are particularly instructive.

Isaac was called Abraham's only son *(yāḥîd. monogenēs),* although Abraham had fathered another male child who was still living. However, the other male offspring, Ishmael, never at any time enjoyed the status of son, as Isaac did. The Code of Hammurabi illuminates this point. Paragraphs 170, 171 show that a man's offspring by a slave woman were not ordinarily given the rights which belonged to the sons borne of his wife. Only if the father in the course of his lifetime had said to the male offspring of his slave woman (in a public and official manner), "Thou art my son," was the slave woman's offspring treated as a real son of the father. If the father had made such a declaration, then the slave woman's offspring was counted among the sons and given an equal share in the inheritance of the father's estate. If no such declaration was made, the offspring of the slave woman were given gifts and separated from the household before the inheritance was divided.

Abraham was evidently at one time eager to legitimize the child of his slave woman and count him as a son and heir. At the incredible announcement that his own wife Sarah would bare a son, he said: "O that Ishmael might live before thee" (Gen. 17:18). But God did not look with favor upon this, and in due course of time, after Sarah gave birth to Isaac, Ishmael was expelled from the household. "Cast out this bondwoman and her son: for the son of this bondwoman shall not be heir with my son, even with Isaac" (Gen. 21:10; Gal. 4:30).

Isaac remained Abraham's only son in the legal sense. Though Abraham had several other offspring (Gen. 25:1-4), he had only one son in the unique sense, and to him he gave his entire inheritance (Gen. 25:5,6). Isaac was his unique son, and when the New Testament refers to Isaac (Heb. 11:17), it calls him his only begotten *(monogenēs).*

It is clear from the above that the expression "only begotten" refers to status. It is certainly used this way of Christ. He has status as the *unique* Son of the Father. The term does not signify that He had a beginning, and the consistent testimony of Scripture is to the contrary; He was and is eternally God's unique Son.

The Term "Begotten"

Psalm 2:7, in a passage that traditionally has been treated as Messianic, reads: " . . . Thou art my Son; this day have I begotten thee." The verse is quoted and applied to Christ three times in the New Testament (Acts 13:33; Heb. 1:5, 5:5), thus introducing the word "begotten" into the doctrine of Christ.

The verb translated "begotten" is used a great number of times in the Old Testament both in the simple (qal) and in the causative (hiphil) conjugations in the ordinary sense of to generate, or to beget, just as anyone familiar with the content of the Old Testament would expect. It appears twenty-eight times in the fifth chapter of Genesis alone in this ordinary sense.

As the verb appears in Psa. 2:7, it is pointed by the

Massoretes as from the simple (qal) conjugation, and is so understood by Gesenius-Kautzsch-Cowley,[6] by Brown, Driver and Briggs, by Franz Delitzsch, and others.

There is no compelling reason, however, why one may not take this verb to be in the causative (hiphil) conjugation. No consonantal changes would be required to so understand it. The causative conjugation is more natural in this context moreover, since its function is not only causative, but declarative. I will show below the necessity of seeing the force of this verb to be declarative. That the causative (hiphil) conjugation sometimes functions as declarative is demonstrated from the following examples:

> *hiṣdîq,*   which means to declare righteous or justify, as in Exod. 23:7; Deut. 25:1; and elsewhere.
>
> *hiršîaʻ,*   which means to declare guilty, or condemn, as in Deut. 25:1; Exod. 22:8 (English, v. 9); Job 9:20; and elsewhere.
>
> *heʻeqîš,*   which in Job 9:20 means to declare perverse.

Taking the verb in Psa. 2:7 to be declarative, i.e., hiphil, that verse may be translated as follows: ". . . Thou art my Son; *this day have I declared thy sonship.*" To understand the verb as declarative removes from it, of course, any necessary reference to beginnings.

Whether one takes the verb translated "begotten" in Psa. 2:7 as hiphil or as some other grammatical form, its meaning in that verse must have to do with the *declaration* of sonship. This assertion is supported by four arguments from Scripture:

(1) *The argument from parallelism.* It is of the nature of Hebrew poetry to phrase itself in parallels. The parallel exhibited in Psa. 2:7 is of the type called synonymous parallelism. In such the idea expressed in the first clause is repeated in the second clause with different vocabulary. In Psa. 2:7 the clause "Thou art my Son" is matched by the

clause "this day have I declared thy sonship," which repeats the same idea.

(2) *The presence of the phrase "this day" (hayyôm).* The day referred to is the day of the declaration of the decree, —the decree which announces the coronation of the king (cf. v. 6). The coronation day could certainly not be the day of the king's generation, but it certainly would be a day in which the proclamation of his sonship would be in order!

(3) *The fact that the New Testament quotes this verse as a prediction of the resurrection.* Acts 13:33,34 refers the words in question, "this day have I begotten thee," not to the incarnation, but to the resurrection of Christ. That being so, the action of that clause must be declarative, for it is the resurrection which declares to all the world that Jesus Christ is the Son of God. As it is stated in Rom. 1:3,4: "Concerning his Son Jesus Christ our Lord, which was made of the seed of David according to the flesh; and *declared to be the Son of God with power,* according to the spirit of holiness, *by the resurrection from the dead."*

(4) *The content of the following verse (Psa. 2:8) requires such an interpretation.* Verse 8 has to do with the inheritance rights of the Son, who is to have the nations for his inheritance and the uttermost parts of the earth for his possession. Now it has been shown above that formal recognition of sonship was a prerequisite of heirship. The Son of God, whose sonship has been publicly declared by means of the resurrection, is constituted the proper heir to the nations of this world.

The fifth chapter of the Revelation depicts in a vision the Son's acceptance of his heirship, offered to him in Psa. 2:8. There one beholds the Lamb that was slain (and thereafter resurrected) step forward and receive that seven-sealed book, the inheritance document of the nations, and thus assume heirship of the world. When this vision shall have become a reality, then shall it be said, "The kingdoms of this world are become the kingdoms of our Lord, and of his Christ; and he shall reign for ever and ever" (Rev. 11:15).

The above arguments show that the verb translated "begotten" in Psa. 2:7 does not refer to generation. The terms "firstborn," "only begotten," and " begotten," as used in the Old and New Testaments concerning Jesus Christ, do not contradict, but are in harmony with, what has been written concerning the meaning of the word "son" as applied to him. The terms "son," "firstborn," "only begotten," and "begotten," as defined by the Bible's own use of them, all declare that Jesus is the uncreated, ungenerated, co-eternal, co-equal Son of God the Father.

DOCUMENTATION

1. William G. T. Shedd, *A History of Christian Doctrine* (New York: Charles Scribner and Co., 1871), I, 294.
2. *Ibid.* Cf. Philip Schaff, *The Creeds of Christendom* (New York: Harper and Brothers, 6th ed., 1931), I, 29.
3. Conveniently consulted in English translation in *Ancient Near Eastern Texts Relating to the Old Testament,* ed. by James B. Pritchard, 2nd ed. (Princeton University Press, Princeton, N. J., 1955), p. 174.
4. *Ibid.,* p. 175.
5. Collected in the author's unpublished (except by microfilm) doctoral dissertation, *Systems of Land Tenure in Ancient Israel* (University of Michigan, 1963), pp. 26- 35.
6. *Gesenius' Hebrew Grammar,* ed. by E. Kautzsch (28th German ed.), trans. by A. E. Cowley, 2nd English ed. (London: Oxford University Press, 1910), p. 120.

APPENDIX B

THE TESTIMONY OF MEN

And we believe and are sure that thou art that Christ, the Son of the living God (John 6:69).

We fully recognize that the testimony of God is infinitely greater than the testimony of men (1 John 5:9). God's Word is our infallible and final authority in determining the nature of Christ's Sonship. It is of interest, however, to consider what respected Bible teachers have written on the subject of eternal Sonship.

John N. Darby, one of the early Plymouth Brethren, devoted Bible student, and prolific author:

> The eternal Sonship is a vital truth, or else we lose the Father sending the Son, and the Son creating, and we have no Father if we have no Son, so that it [the doctrine of eternal Sonship] lies at the basis of all truth. . . . I hold it vital to hold the Sonship before the worlds. It is the truth.[1]

C. H. Mackintosh, highly esteemed Plymouth Brethren author and preacher:

> I would, at this point, solemnly admonish my reader that he cannot be too jealous in reference to the vital truth of the Person and the relations of the Lord Jesus Christ. If there be error as to this, there is no security

as to any thing. God cannot give the sanction of His presence to aught that has not this truth for its foundation. The Person of Christ is the living, divine centre round which the Holy Ghost carries on all His operations. Let slip the truth as to Him, and you are like a vessel broken from its moorings, and carried, without rudder or compass, over the wild watery waste, and in imminent danger of being dashed to fragments upon the rocks of Arianism, infidelity, or atheism. Question the eternal Sonship of Christ, question His deity, question His unspotted humanity, and you have opened the floodgate for a desolating tide of deadly error to rush in. Let no one imagine, for a moment, that this is a mere matter to be discussed by learned theologians—a curious question—a recondite mystery—a point about which we may lawfully differ. No; it is a vital, fundamental truth, to be held in the power of the Holy Ghost, and maintained at the expense of all beside—yea, to be confessed under all circumstances, whatever may be the consequences.[2]

We rejoice in every opportunity for the setting forth of Christ's Eternal Sonship. We hold it to be an integral and essentially necessary part of the Christian faith.[3]

Charles Spurgeon, author, English Baptist preacher, pastor of Metropolitan Tabernacle in London:

But Jesus, the eternal Son of God, "very God of very God," who had been hymned through eternal ages by joyous angels, who had been the favourite of his Father's court, exalted high above principalities and powers, and every name that is named, he himself condescended to become man; was born of the Virgin Mary; was cradled in a manger; lived a life of suffering, and at last died a death of agony.[4]

Question 20: Who is the Redeemer of God's elect?
Answer: The only Redeemer of God's elect is the
Lord Jesus Christ, who being the eternal Son of God,
became man, and so was and continues to be God and
man, in two distinct natures and one person for ever.[5]

H. A. Ironside, author, beloved Bible teacher, pastor of
Moody Church in Chicago:

> More recently the so-called Raven meetings have
> been divided over the teaching of an American
> leader who denied the truth of the Eternal Sonship
> of Christ. This most serious error caused many to
> take a definite stand against it and led to another
> separation. But sadly enough by far the greater
> majority saw nothing wrong in such views and have
> gone on with the promulgator of them. This puts
> these meetings entirely off the ground of the early
> Brethren who considered a true confession of Christ
> the very first consideration.[6]

T. Ernest Wilson, author and missionary to Angola for
nearly half a century:

> The eternal Sonship of Christ is one of the most
> vital, basic doctrines of the Word of God. It is denied
> by many heretical cults, but held and valued by all
> those who know and love our Lord Jesus Christ . . .
> we must be on guard against those who say that He
> only became the Son of God at His incarnation and
> who deny His eternal Sonship.[7]

Charles Hodge, American Presbyterian theologian:

> The [Nicene] Council declared that our Lord is the
> Eternal Son of God, i.e., that He is from eternity the

Son of God. This of course involves the denial that He became the Son of God in time; and consequently, that the primary and essential reason for his being called Son is not his miraculous birth, nor his incarnation, nor his resurrection, nor his exaltation to the right hand of God. The Council decided that the word Son as applied to Christ, is not a term of office but of nature; that it expresses the relation which the Second Person in the Trinity from eternity bears to the First Person, and that the relation thus indicated is sameness of nature, so that Sonship, in the case of Christ, includes equality with God.[8]

The word Son [in Romans 1:3-4] designates the divine nature of Christ. In all cases, however, it is a designation implying participation of the divine nature. Christ is called the Son of God because he is consubstantial with the Father, and therefore equal to him in power and glory. The term expresses the relation of the second to the first person in the Trinity, as it exists from eternity. It is therefore, as applied to Christ, not a term of office, nor expressive of any relation assumed in time. He was and is the Eternal Son.[9]

Augustus H. Strong, Baptist minister and theologian:

The Sonship of Christ is eternal . . . neither the incarnation, the baptism, the transfiguration, nor the resurrection marks the beginning of Christ's Sonship, or constitutes him the Son of God. These are but recognitions or manifestations of a pre-existing Sonship, inseparable from his Godhood. . . . Not a commencement of existence, but an eternal relation to the Father—there never having been a time when the Son began to be, or when the Son did not exist as God with the Father.[10]

Benjamin B. Warfield, eminent Presbyterian theologian and educator and seminary president:

> The designation "Son of God" is a metaphysical designation and tells us what He is in His being of being. And what it tells us that Christ is in His being of being is that He is just what God is. It is undeniable—and Bousset, for example, does not deny it,—that, from the earliest days of Christianity on, (in Bousset's words) "Son of God was equivalent simply to equal with God" (Mark xiv. 61-63; John x. 31-39).[11]
>
> We read that "When the fulness of the time came, God sent forth his Son, born of a woman, born under the law, that he might redeem them that were under the law." The whole transaction is referred to the Father in fulfillment of His eternal plan of redemption, and it is described specifically as an incarnation: the Son of God is born of a woman—He who is in His own nature the Son of God, abiding with God, is sent forth from God in such a manner as to be born a human being, subject to law. The primary implications are that this was not the beginning of His being; but that before this He was neither a man nor subject to law. But there is no suggestion that on becoming man and subject to law, He ceased to be the Son of God or lost anything intimated by that high designation. The uniqueness of His relation to God as His Son is emphasized in a kindred passage (Rom. viii. 3) by the heightening of the designation to that of God's "own Son."[12]

John Murray, professor of systematic theology at Westminster Seminary for thirty-six years:

> There are people, while not being in anyway disposed to the denial of Jesus' deity, who maintain the title "Son of God" is solely a Messianic title, a title

that belongs to Him in virtue of His incarnation. It is that position that I am trying to contradict to a very large extent....the title "Son of God" is applied to Him in virtue of His pretemporal, ontological, intertrinitarian relationship identity.

Now, since He came from above—from heaven, from the Father—it was in the identity that was His in heaven and with the Father prior to His coming that He came and was sent. This identity is distinctly specified as that of Son, and "only begotten." Hence, His filial identity, I submit, is preexistent, pretemporal and transcendent.[13]

There are good reasons for thinking that in this instance [Romans 1:3-4] the title ["Son"] refers to a relation which the Son sustains to the Father antecedently to and independently of his manifestation in the flesh. Paul entertained the highest conception of Christ in his divine identity and eternal preexistence. The title "Son" he regarded as applicable to Christ in his eternal preexistence and as defining his eternal relation to the Father. . . . the subject matter of the gospel is defined as that which pertains to the eternal Son of God.[14]

J. Oliver Buswell, college and seminary professor of theology for many years:

The virgin birth of Christ was a miracle wrought by the Third Person of the Trinity whereby the Second Person of the Trinity, the eternal Son of God, took to Himself a human nature, so that He "became man" . . . . what then shall we say of eternal Sonship? . . . There can be no doubt that "Father, Son, and Holy Spirit" are words intended by the writers of the Scriptures to indicate eternal relationships within the Triune Godhead.[15]

Loraine Boettner, respected theologian:

> In theological language the terms "Father" and "Son" carry with them not our occidental ideas of, on the one hand, source of being and superiority, and on the other, subordination and dependence, but rather the Semitic and oriental ideas of likeness or sameness of nature and equality of being. It is, of course, the Semitic consciousness that underlies the phraseology of Scripture, and wherever the Scriptures call Christ the 'Son of God' they assert His true and proper deity.... As any merely human son is like his father in his essential nature, that is, possessed of humanity, so Christ, the Son of God, was like His Father in His essential nature, that is, possessed of deity. The Father and the Son, together with the Holy Spirit, are coeternal and coequal in power and glory, and partake of the same nature or substance.[16]

C. I. Scofield, dispensational author and Bible teacher, founder of the Central American Mission:

> God is the Father of our Lord Jesus Christ. This relation, in some sense not clearly explained, is fundamental in the divine Being and always existed. Although in His incarnation our Lord became a true human being, at the same time He continued to be "the Son of God."[17]

Lewis Sperry Chafer, dispensational theologian and founder of Dallas Theological Seminary:

> He was the Son of God from all eternity, but He became Son of man by incarnation . . . various theories which contend that Christ was: (a) Son of

God by virtue of incarnation; (b) that He was Son of God by virtue of His resurrection; or (c) that He was Son of God by mere title or official position, break down before the volume of Biblical testimony which asserts that He was Son of God from all eternity.[18]

E. Schuyler English, author, editor of *Our Hope* magazine, chairman of the editorial committee of the *New Scofield Reference Bible.*

The Father has always been the Father; the Son has always been the Son; the Holy Spirit has always been the Holy Spirit.... And of the Son it is written, "Jesus Christ the same yesterday, and today, and for ever" (Heb. 13:8). He always was God the Son; He continued to be God the Son in His earthly garb as Man; He remains God the Son, as He shall always be, in His heavenly exaltation.[19]

Lehman Strauss, author, widely traveled dispensational Bible teacher:

Every claim of Jesus Christ, including the confessions of other men, that He was the Son of God is a remarkable expression that shows the eternal relationship between the Father and the Son. His title of Son of God is not based upon His Virgin Birth. He did not become the Son of God by virtue of His birth in the manger of Bethlehem, but He was Son of God by inherent right in eternity past. . . . There is no support in favor of the doctrine that the divine relationship between the Father and the Son had its beginning at the Incarnation. . . . There was never a time when this relationship between the Father and the Son had a beginning. The title of this chapter might well be "The *Eternal* Sonship of Christ."[20]

Robert P. Lightner, author, professor of systematic theology at Dallas Theological Seminary:

> The term "Son of God" describes the Savior's relationship to God the Father. His relationship to God is eternal and was not affected by the incarnation. "Son of God" is not less, but far more than a name or title. It is another way of setting Christ forth as the only begotten. The second member of the Godhead did become the Son of man, the son of David, and the son of Mary when He became incarnate but He was the Son of God from all eternity.[21]

John F. Walvoord, author, theologian, and for many years president of Dallas Theological Seminary:

> The consensus of the great theologians of the church and the great church councils is to the effect that Christ has been a Son from eternity; and the theory that He became a Son by incarnation is inadequate to account for the usage of the term. . . . The Scriptures represent Christ as eternally the Son of God by eternal generation. While it must be admitted that the nature of the generation is unique, being eternal, sonship has been used in the Bible to represent the relationship between the first Person and the second Person. . . . The scriptural view of the sonship of Christ, as recognized in many of the great creeds of the church, is that Christ was always the Son of God.[22]

NOTES

Foreword

1. See note 12 under chapter 5.

Preface

1. H. A. Ironside, *A Historical Sketch of the Brethren Movement* (Neptune, New Jersey: Loizeaux, 1985) 131.

Chapter 1

1. Unbelieving scholarship often employs an ingenious repunctuation scheme in an effort to rob Romans 9:5 of its clear testimony to the deity of Christ. This has been answered in an article entitled "A Suggested Method for Evaluating Bible Translations—An Examination of Romans 9:5" by George Zeller, which appeared in *The Voice*, a publication of the Independent Fundamental Churches of America (July/August 1979): 3,5-6.
2. The Greek construction of 2 Peter 1:1 (the Granville Sharp rule) demands that we understand the term *God* to be referring not to God the Father but to "our Savior Jesus Christ." This same construction is found in Titus 2:13, where "the great God" is none other than Jesus Christ.
3. The word *Lord* in Philippians 2:11 is the Greek word *kurios,* which is consistently used in the Septuagint (ancient Greek version of the Old Testament) in translating the Hebrew word *Jehovah.*
4. Jehovah's Witnesses deny the deity of Christ and teach that Jesus is a mighty angelic creature who was created by Jehovah God. They strongly maintain that the divine name *Jehovah* is never used of Christ.
5. A more detailed defense of the doctrine of the deity of Christ, based on the excellent notes of the late Dr. Alva McClain, is available from the Middletown Bible Church, 349 East Street, Middletown, CT 06457.

Chapter 4

1. If it can be demonstrated that Christ existed as the Son prior to the incarnation, the arguments of those who teach that His Sonship began at His baptism or resurrection or exaltation will be answered as well.
2. John C. Whitcomb, *Daniel.* Copyright 1985. Moody Bible Institute of Chicago. Moody Press. p. 60. Dr. Whitcomb identifies this fourth person as the preincarnate Son of God even though he says that "Nebuchadnezzar would not have been capable of identifying God's Son even if he did see Him." Used by permission.

Chapter 5

1. R. A. Huebner, *F. E. Raven's Evil Doctrines* (Morganville, NJ: Present Truth, 1980) 26.
2. Raven's heresies surfaced after Darby's death, but the writings and letters of Darby reveal that Darby himself was a strong defender of eternal Sonship, considering this truth "vital" (see appendix B). In addition to his denial of eternal Sonship, Raven also held other strange and unorthodox views, especially regarding the person of Christ and eternal life. See Huebner's book cited above for a detailed discussion of Raven's teachings.
3. J. C. Philpot, *The True, Proper, and Eternal Sonship of the Lord Jesus Christ, The Only Begotten Son of God* (England: Gospel Standard Baptist Trust, 1926 reprint).
4. See for example Ralph Wardlaw, *Systematic Theology* (Edinburgh: Black, 1857) 2:32-60.
5. Adam Clarke and Albert Barnes are two examples of commentators who taught Sonship by means of incarnation, although it is interesting that the editor of *Barnes' Notes,* Robert Frew, strongly disagreed with this position and countered it in the footnotes. See Barnes' comments on Romans 1:4 (*Barnes' Notes,* Grand Rapids: Baker, 1985 reprint) and Clarke's comments on Luke 1:35 (*Commentary on the Whole Bible,* London: Thomas Tagg and Son, 1838).
6. Jimmy Swaggart's strong denial of eternal Sonship is documented in *The Biblical Evangelist* (November 1, 1987): 7, ed. Dr. Robert L. Sumner, P. O. Box Drawer 940, Ingleside, TX 78362. Swaggart, according to this article, teaches that the doctrine of eternal Sonship is erroneous and contrary to Scripture. He says that God's Son did have a beginning when

Mary gave birth to Jesus. Also see the August 1980 issue of Swaggart's magazine *The Evangelist* for further documentation.

7. Finis Jennings Dake, *Dake's Annotated Reference Bible* (Lawrenceville, GA: Dake Bible Sales, 1963) 139 (N.T.).

8. Walter Martin, *The Kingdom of the Cults* (Minneapolis: Bethany House, 1985) 117-118.

9. Taken from: *The MacArthur New Testament Commentary— Hebrews* by John MacArthur, Jr. Copyright 1983. Moody Bible Institute of Chicago. Moody Press. Used by permission. pp. 27-28. See his discussion of Hebrews 1:4-5.

10. Taken from: *The MacArthur New Testament Commentary— Galatians* by John MacArthur, Jr. Copyright 1987. Moody Bible Institute of Chicago. Moody Press. Used by permission. p. 108. See his comments under Galatians 4:4.

11. Taken from: *John MacArthur's Bible Studies—Acting on the Good News (Romans 1:1-16)* by John MacArthur, Jr. Copyright 1987. Moody Bible Institute of Chicago. Moody Press. Used by permission. pp. 35,41. For another clear denial of eternal Sonship see *John MacArthur's Bible Studies—The Superiority of Christ—Hebrews 1–2* (Copyright 1986. Moody Bible Institute of Chicago. Moody Press. pp. 52-54). Dr. MacArthur has also presented his Sonship-by-incarnation view by means of his cassette tape ministry. Two tapes that very clearly set forth his position on Sonship are Tape GC 1602 (Hebrews 1:4-6) and Tape GC 45-3 (Romans 1:2-4), which are distributed by Word of Grace Communications, P. O. Box 4000, Panorama City, CA 91412.

12. I have this letter in my files. My purpose in sharing this is to set forth a position that is being held today. It is not necessary to reveal the identity of the professor who wrote these words. Our concern in this book is to defend the doctrine of eternal Sonship against current denials, not to attack personalities. Some names have been cited in this chapter because these individuals have made their positions known through their published and public writings. "Christian leaders should be held accountable for what they say in books, magazines and pulpit, or on radio or television. Certainly no one can object if what he has stated publicly is quoted or questioned publicly" (Dave Hunt in the Foreword to *PsychoHeresy— The Psychological Seduction of Christianity* by Martin and Deidre Bobgan, Santa Barbara, CA: East Gate, 1987).

Chapter 6

1. W. J. Hocking, *The Son of His Love—Papers on the Eternal Sonship* (Sunbury, PA: Believers Bookshelf, 1970) 87.
2. John Nelson Darby, from a tract on eternal Sonship (no title) published by Present Truth Publishers, 411 Route 79, Morganville, NJ 07751.
3. Hocking, *The Son of His Love*, 127.
4. W. E. Vine, *The Divine Sonship of Christ* (Minneapolis: Klock & Klock, 1984 reprint) 38-39.
5. William Hendriksen, *New Testament Commentary— Exposition of the Gospel According to John* (Grand Rapids: Baker, 1953) 87.
6. J. G. Bellett, *The Son of God* (Addison, IL: Bible Truth, 1978 reprint) 11-12.
7. Ibid., 10.
8. Ibid., 12 (cited by Bellett but no author mentioned).
9. Charles Hodge, *Systematic Theology* (Grand Rapids: Eerdmans, 1979 reprint) 1:473.
10. Vine, *The Divine Sonship*, 27-28.
11. Ibid., part 2, p. 12 (the second part of the book has a different numbering system).
12. See Matthew Henry's comments under John 1:18.
13. This quote is taken from editorial comments under Romans 1:4 in *Barnes' Notes*, 17.
14. See Vine's discussion in *The Divine Sonship*, 8-9.
15. Philpot, *The True, Proper, and Eternal Sonship*, 32.
16. Ibid., 34.
17. Vine, *The Divine Sonship*, 11.
18. Philpot, *The True, Proper, and Eternal Sonship*, 30.
19. Hocking, *The Son of His Love*, 36-37.
20. Vine, *The Divine Sonship*, 54-55.
21. Ibid., 52.
22. Ibid., 10.
23. Benjamin Breckinridge Warfield, *The Person and Work of Christ* (Philadelphia: Presbyterian and Reformed, 1970) 81.
24. Taken from the doctrinal statement of the Independent Fundamental Churches of America.
25. The wondrous manifestation of the Son of God in connection with His entrance into this world is also taught in John 11:27 and 1 John 5:20.
26. Hocking, *The Son of His Love*, 136-137.
27. Vine, *The Divine Sonship*, part 2, pp. 16-17.

Chapter 7

1. F. F. Bruce, *Commentary on the Epistle to the Hebrews* (Grand Rapids: Eerdmans, 1964) 57-58.
2. Eduard Lohse, "huios," *Theological Dictionary of the New Testament,* Vol. VIII ed. Gerhard Friedrich, trans. and ed. Geoffrey W. Bromiley (Grand Rapids: Eerdmans, 1972) 358.
3. Carsten Colpe, "ho huios tou anthropou," *Theological Dictionary of the New Testament,* VIII:406.
4. Hermann Cremer, "huios," *Biblico-Theological Lexicon of New Testament Greek,* trans. William Urwick (Edinburgh: T. & T. Clark, 1895) 559.
5. Vine, *An Expository Dictionary of New Testament Words* (Old Tappan, NJ: Revell, 1966) IV:50.
6. Lawrence O. Richards, "son," *Expository Dictionary of Bible Words* (Grand Rapids: Zondervan, 1985) 574.
7. William F. Arndt and F. Wilbur Gingrich, *A Greek-English Lexicon of the New Testament,* 4th rev. ed. (Chicago: The University of Chicago Press, 1957) 884.
8. Gerhard Kelber, "charakter," *Theological Dictionary of the New Testament,* Vol. IX ed. Gerhard Friedrich, trans. and ed. Geoffrey W. Bromiley (Grand Rapids: Eerdmans, 1974) 420.
9. Arndt and Gingrich, *Greek-English Lexicon,* 854.
10. Kelber, *Theological Dictionary of the New Testament,* IX:422.
11. Friedrich Buchsel, "monogenes," *Theological Dictionary of the New Testament,* Vol. IV ed. Gerhard Kittel, trans. and ed. Geoffrey W. Bromiley (Grand Rapids: Eerdmans, 1967) 739.
12. Arndt and Gingrich, *Greek-English Lexicon,* 370.
13. Wilhelm Schneemelcher, "huios," *Theological Dictionary of the New Testament,* VIII:387.
14. Vine, *An Expository Dictionary,* IV:48.

Chapter 8

1. Bruce, *Commentary on the Book of Acts* (Grand Rapids: Eerdmans, 1954) 489-90.
2. Francis Brown, S. R. Driver, and Charles A. Briggs, "yalad," *A Hebrew and English Lexicon of the Old Testament* (Oxford: Clarendon, 1975) 408.
3. Georg Bertram, "odin," *Theological Dictionary of the New Testament,* IX:670.
4. Ibid.
5. Ibid., 671.
6. Ibid., 671-72.

7. Ibid., 673.
8. Martin Hengel, *Crucifixion* (Philadelphia: Fortress, 1977) 22-32.
9. Cicero, as quoted by Hengel in *Crucifixion,* 8.
10. Ibid., 42.
11. Josephus, as quoted by Hengel in *Crucifixion,* 8.
12. Hengel, *Crucifixion,* 33-38.
13. Ibid., 46-63.
14. Ibid., 1-10.
15. Ibid., 7.
16. Celsus, as quoted by Hengel in *Crucifixion,* 17.
17. Hengel, *Crucifixion,* 6-7.
18. Ibid., 10.

Chapter 9

1. Such able exegetes as John Murray and Charles Hodge both recognize that Paul in Romans 1:3-4 was affirming Christ's essential and eternal Sonship. This material is cited in appendix B.
2. Taken from *Hebrews Verse By Verse* by William R. Newell. Copyright 1947. Moody Bible Institute of Chicago. Moody Press. Used by permission. p. 21 (including footnote).
3. Compare the doctrinal statement of the Independent Fundamental Churches of America: "We believe that the Lord Jesus Christ, the eternal Son of God, became Man without ceasing to be God."
4. In his *Commentary on the Gospel of Luke* (Grand Rapids: Eerdmans, 1951) Norval Geldenhuys insists on eternal Sonship in Luke 1:35,38.
5. Charles Bridges, *Proverbs* (Edinburgh: Banner of Truth, 1968 reprint) 591-592. See also the discussion of Proverbs 30:4 in Dr. Arnold Fruchtenbaum's book entitled *Jesus Was A Jew* (Ariel Ministries, 1981) 61-62.
6. See comments by Dr. Showers in chapter 8 about the New Testament use of Psalm 2:7.
7. See the discussion by Dr. Showers in chapter 7 regarding the significance of the phrase *Son of God.*
8. Hocking, *The Son of His Love,* 148.
9. Ibid., 146-147.
10. See the helpful discussion by Philpot in *The True, Proper, and Eternal Sonship,* 35.
11. W. J. Ouweneel, *What Is The Eternal Sonship of Christ?* (Sunbury, PA: Believers Bookshelf, 1976) 16-17.

12. For a helpful discussion of eternal generation see J. Oliver Buswell's *A Systematic Theology of the Christian Religion* (Grand Rapids: Zondervan, 1972) 1:112. Also see editor Robert Frew's footnotes that accompany the commentary on Romans 1 in *Barnes' Notes,* 16.

Chapter 10

1. For an insightful look at the controversy in the Brethren assemblies, see Huebner's book cited above.
2. Philip Schaff, *History of the Christian Church* (Grand Rapids: Eerdmans, 1910) VIII:783.
3. Ibid., 785.
4. We insist that **no** human being in the church age should **ever** be executed for **any** spiritual or theological error. At the same time, we dare not minimize doctrinal errors and must be careful to apply New Testament principles of Biblical separation and church discipline.
5. MacArthur, *Our Sufficiency in Christ* (Dallas: Word, 1991) 170.
6. MacArthur, *Charismatic Chaos* (Grand Rapids: Zondervan, 1992) 14-15.
7. The former director of this mission wrote of the doctrinal struggle that took place as the result of his change in position with respect to the rapture. See Marvin Rosenthal, *The Pre-Wrath Rapture of the Church* (Nashville: Nelson, 1990) chapter 1, 17-36.
8. Compare John MacArthur's statements published in the booklet *The Sonship of Christ* (Grandville, MI: IFCA Press, November 1991) with the official doctrinal statement of the Independent Fundamental Churches of America, which declares that the Lord Jesus Christ is "the eternal Son of God."
9. Norman L. Geisler wrote these words in an open letter entitled "Why I Left the Evangelical Free Church Ministerial," July 5, 1988.
10. Fuller Seminary's departure from the doctrine of Biblical inerrancy is well-documented in Harold Lindsell's book *The Battle For the Bible* (Grand Rapids: Zondervan, 1976) chapter 6, 106-121.
11. Ironside, "Exposing Error—Is It Worthwhile?" *The Gospel Standard* (March 1992) 4.
12. We have already established the fact that the Bible teaches that the second person of the triune God has eternally existed as the Son. See especially chapters 4 and 6.

13. My thanks to Miles Stanford, author of *The Complete Green Letters,* for his unpublished study on eternal Sonship that has provided helpful insight into these matters.
14. John F. Walvoord, *Jesus Christ Our Lord* (Chicago: Moody Press, 1969) 39.
15. See the helpful discussion in F. W. Grant's, *The Crowned Christ* (Sunbury, PA: Believers Bookshelf, 1984 reprint) 21.
16. Walvoord, *Jesus Christ Our Lord,* 39.
17. The doctrinal statement of the Independent Fundamental Churches of America says it this way: "We believe in one Triune God, eternally existing in three Persons—Father, Son, and Holy Spirit."
18. Philpot, *The True, Proper, and Eternal Sonship,* 31,39-40.

Appendix B

1. John Nelson Darby quote is taken from "The Son of Man," which appears in *Notes and Comments,* II:423, and in a tract published by Present Truth Publishers, 411 Route 79, Morganville, NJ 07751.
2. C. H. Mackintosh, *Genesis to Deuteronomy* (Neptune, NJ: Loizeaux, 1972) 295.
3. This quote is found on the back cover of the book by W. R. Dronsfield entitled *The Eternal Son of the Father* (London: Chapter Two, 1987). The date of the quote is given as 1873 but the original source is not indicated.
4. Charles H. Spurgeon, *The New Park Street Pulpit* (Pasadena, TX: Pilgrim, 1975) 5:243. Quote is from Spurgeon's sermon, "Justice Satisfied," delivered on May 29, 1859.
5. Spurgeon, *A Catechism With Proofs* (Pasadena, TX: Pilgrim, 1985) 9.
6. Ironside, *A Historical Sketch,* 131.
7. T. Ernest Wilson, *The Messianic Psalms* (Neptune, NJ: Loizeaux, 1978) 16-17.
8. Hodge, *Systematic Theology,* 1:471.
9. Hodge, *Commentary on the Epistle to the Romans,* paperback edition (Grand Rapids: Eerdmans, 1976) 18.
10. Augustus Hopkins Strong, *Systematic Theology* (Philadelphia: Judson, 1907) 340.
11. Warfield, *The Person and Work of Christ,* 77.
12. Ibid., 45. Also see Warfield's discussion of Romans 1:3-4 cited in chapter 6.
13. This quote is taken from a transcription of a message given by

John Murray entitled "Eternal Sonship." The tape is cataloged as JM-205 and is available from Westminster Media, P.O. Box 27009, Philadelphia, PA 19118. This message presents several well-reasoned arguments in favor of the doctrine of eternal Sonship.
14. John Murray, *The Epistle to the Romans,* one-volume edition (Grand Rapids: Eerdmans, 1968) 5.
15. Buswell, *A Systematic Theology,* 1:107,112.
16. Loraine Boettner, *Studies in Theology* (Grand Rapids: Eerdmans, 1947) 152-153.
17. Taken from: *The Scofield Correspondence Course* by C. I. Scofield. Copyright 1959. Moody Bible Institute of Chicago. Moody Press. Used by permission. VI:1482.
18. Lewis Sperry Chafer, *Systematic Theology* (Dallas: Dallas Seminary Press, 1948) VII:290; III:30.
19. E. Schuyler English, *Things Surely To Be Believed* (Neptune, NJ: Loizeaux, 1956) 24,44-45.
20. Lehman Strauss, *The Godhead* (Neptune, NJ: Loizeaux, 1990) 256-257.
21. Robert P. Lightner, *Sin, the Savior and Salvation—The Theology of Everlasting Life* (Nashville: Nelson, 1991) 55.
22. Taken from: *Jesus Christ Our Lord* by John F. Walvoord. Copyright 1969. Moody Bible Institute of Chicago. Moody Press. Used by permission. pp. 39,41-42.

RESOURCES FOR FURTHER STUDY

Books

Bellett, J. G. *The Son of God.* Reprint. Addison, IL: Bible Truth, 1978.

Dronsfield, W. R. *The Eternal Son of the Father.* London: Chapter Two, 1987. Available through Believers Bookshelf, Box 261, Sunbury, PA 17801.

Hocking, W. J. *The Son of His Love—Papers on The Eternal Sonship.* Sunbury, PA: Believers Bookshelf, 1970.

Lightner, Robert P. *Sin, the Savior and Salvation—The Theology of Everlasting Life.* Nashville: Nelson, 1991. This volume is not being reprinted, but it is available from the author, c/o Dallas Theological Seminary, 3909 Swiss Ave., Dallas, TX 75204.

Ouweneel, W. J. *What Is The Eternal Sonship of Christ?* Sunbury, PA: Believers Bookshelf, 1976.

Ross, Bob L., *The Trinity and the Eternal Sonship of Christ--A Defense Against "Oneness" Pentecostal Attacks on Historic Christianity.* Pasadena, TX: Pilgrim, 1993. The address of Pilgrim Publications is P.O. Box 66, Pasadena, TX 77501.

Vine, W. E. *The Divine Sonship of Christ.* Reprint. Minneapolis: Klock & Klock, 1984.

Walvoord, John F. *Jesus Christ Our Lord.* Chicago: Moody Press, 1969.

Cassette tapes

Lightner, Robert and Showers, Renald. "God the Eternal Son," a series of five tapes of messages delivered at an IFCA meeting in Aberdeen, Maryland, on September 24, 1991. Available from Bright Spot Bookstore, P.O. Box 878, Aberdeen, MD 21001. Cost for all 5 tapes: $7.00 (price includes postage).

Murray, John. "Eternal Sonship," Tape JM-205. Available from Westminster Media, P.O. Box 27009, Philadelphia, PA 19118. Cost: $6.00 (price includes postage).